Praise for *The Persuasion Engine*

"With great insight and compelling examples, Roger Dooley shows entrepreneurs how to use AI, neuromarketing, and behavioral science to punch far above their weight."

—**Robert Cialdini,**
Author of *Influence* and *Pre-Suasion*

"A masterclass in what actually drives behavior in the age of AI. *The Persuasion Engine* shows how to apply behavioral science and AI together—ethically and practically—to influence decisions that stick."

—**Nir Eyal,**
Author of *Hooked*, *Indistractable*, and *Beyond Belief*

"The Persuasion Engine is a clear, practical guide to what truly drives customer decisions. Roger Dooley demystifies neuromarketing and translates behavioral science into usable insights that help marketers create messages that connect emotionally and inspire action. Smart, grounded, and immediately applicable, this book is essential reading for anyone who wants to stop guessing, understand their customers more deeply, and build marketing that actually works."

—**Marshall Goldsmith,**
Thinkers50 #1 Executive Coach and
New York Times bestselling author of
The Earned Life, Triggers, and *What Got You Here Won't Get You There*

"Emotions drive decisions, and in this essential book Roger Dooley shows how scalable, low-cost neuroscience tools let marketers measure emotion and create experiences that truly delight customers."

—**Paul J. Zak, PhD,**
Founder, Immersion Neuroscience and Author of
The Little Book of Happiness: A Scientific Approach to Living Better

"This is the marketing equivalent of *The Imitation Game*—decoding the often bizarre and hard-to-predict mass of internal wiring which lies between objective reality and human behaviour."

—Rory Sutherland,
Vice Chairman, Ogilvy

"Required reading for every company that intends to thrive in the age of AI."

—Nancy Harhut,
Author of *Using Behavioral Science in Marketing*

"Roger has been a go-to expert in my career for many years. This new masterpiece turns AI and behavioral science into actionable business tactics."

—Mark Schaefer,
Author of *How AI Changes Your Customers*

"Roger Dooley has leveled the playing field, giving every business owner the 'big enterprise' tools they need to outsmart and out-influence the giants. Bonus: No budget necessary!"

—Mike Michalowicz,
Author of *The Money Habit and Profit First*

"The Persuasion Engine is a must-read, as the powers of persuasion have been forever altered in the new universe of modern work."

—Nir Bashan,
Author of *The Solution Mindset* and International Keynote Speaker

"This book will put some small marketing agencies out of business, unless they lean in and use every idea."

—Dr. Diane Dye,
Author of *Creating Critical Opportunity*

THE PERSUASION ENGINE

"A masterclass in what actually drives behavior in the age of AI."
—**Nir Eyal**, author of *Hooked*, *Indistractable*, and *Beyond Belief*

THE PERSUASION ENGINE

HOW **ANY BUSINESS** CAN USE **AI-POWERED NEUROMARKETING** TO **UNDERSTAND** AND **WIN CUSTOMERS**

ROGER DOOLEY
Author of *Brainfluence* and *Friction*

WILEY

Copyright © 2026 by Roger Dooley. All rights reserved.

Published by John Wiley & Sons, Inc., Hoboken, New Jersey.

No part of this publication may be reproduced, stored in a retrieval system, or transmitted in any form or by any means, electronic, mechanical, photocopying, recording, scanning, or otherwise, except as permitted under Section 107 or 108 of the 1976 United States Copyright Act, without either the prior written permission of the Publisher, or authorization through payment of the appropriate per-copy fee to the Copyright Clearance Center, Inc., 222 Rosewood Drive, Danvers, MA 01923, (978) 750-8400, fax (978) 750-4470, or on the web at www.copyright.com. Requests to the Publisher for permission should be addressed to the Permissions Department, John Wiley & Sons, Inc., 111 River Street, Hoboken, NJ 07030, (201) 748-6011, fax (201) 748-6008, or online at http://www.wiley.com/go/permission.

The manufacturer's authorized representative according to the EU General Product Safety Regulation is Wiley-VCH GmbH, Boschstr. 12, 69469 Weinheim, Germany, e-mail: Product_Safety@wiley.com.

Trademarks: Wiley and the Wiley logo are trademarks or registered trademarks of John Wiley & Sons, Inc. and/or its affiliates in the United States and other countries and may not be used without written permission. All other trademarks are the property of their respective owners. John Wiley & Sons, Inc. is not associated with any product or vendor mentioned in this book.

Limit of Liability/Disclaimer of Warranty: While the publisher and the authors have used their best efforts in preparing this work, including a review of the content of the work, neither the publisher nor the authors make any representations or warranties with respect to the accuracy or completeness of the contents of this work and specifically disclaim all warranties, including without limitation any implied warranties of merchantability or fitness for a particular purpose. No warranty may be created or extended by sales representatives, written sales materials or promotional statements for this work. The fact that an organization, website, or product is referred to in this work as a citation and/or potential source of further information does not mean that the publisher and authors endorse the information or services the organization, website, or product may provide or recommendations it may make. This work is sold with the understanding that the publisher is not engaged in rendering professional services. The advice and strategies contained herein may not be suitable for your situation. You should consult with a specialist where appropriate. Further, readers should be aware that websites listed in this work may have changed or disappeared between when this work was written and when it is read. Neither the publisher nor authors shall be liable for any loss of profit or any other commercial damages, including but not limited to special, incidental, consequential, or other damages.

For general information on our other products and services or for technical support, please contact our Customer Care Department within the United States at (800) 762-2974, outside the United States at (317) 572-3993 or fax (317) 572-4002.

Wiley also publishes its books in a variety of electronic formats. Some content that appears in print may not be available in electronic formats. For more information about Wiley products, visit our web site at www.wiley.com.

Library of Congress Cataloging-in-Publication Data is Available:

ISBN 9781394383252 (Cloth)
ISBN 9781394383269 (ePub)
ISBN 9781394383276 (ePDF)

Cover Design: Wiley
Cover Image: © ilyast/Getty Images
Author Photo: © Robert Sky Bradshaw
SKY10149644_031726

*For Andrew, Owen, and Zoe—may you shape
the future with wisdom and wonder.*

Contents

Introduction — xix

PART I THE FUTURE OF MARKETING IS HERE — 1

1 A Short History of Neuromarketing — 3
Why Neuromarketing Is Important — 3
Neuroscience and Marketing? — 5
Neuromarketing Through the Years — 5
Behavioral Science for All — 6
The Pandemic Push — 6
The AI Transformation — 7
Neuromarketing 2.0 — 7

PART II THE NEW TOOLS OF NEUROMARKETING — 9

2 Eye-Tracking Revolution — 11
Which Book Cover Gets Attention? — 12
    My Experiment: Book Covers in Online Stores — 12
    Can Less Expensive, Faster Techniques Work? — 14
    The Experiment Continues: Device Camera Eye Tracking — 14
    Who Needs Humans? — 15

Repeating the Book Experiment with AI Eye-Tracking Simulators	16
Book Experiment Takeaway	17
Remote Eye Tracking	17
Limitations of Remote Eye Tracking	18
How to Use Remote Eye Tracking	18
AI Eye-Tracking Simulators	19
Pros and Cons of AI Eye Tracking	21
Data vs. Guessing	21
A Big Caution	22
The Power of Fast Iteration	22
How to Get Started with AI Eye Tracking	23
What's Next	24

3 Facial Coding — 25

Remote, Real-Time Facial Coding	25
Limitations of Device Camera Facial Coding	26
How to Use Facial Coding	27
What's Next	28

4 Biometrics Everywhere — 29

The Wearable Revolution	29
The Advantages of Wearables	30
Barriers to Wearables	30
Immersion Neuroscience: Real-World Biometrics Made Simple	31
From DARPA Labs to Your Wrist	31
What Can You Measure?	32
How to Get Started	33
Limitations of Immersion	34
Pairing Immersion with Other Methods	34
What's Next	35

5	**Implicit Testing**	**37**
	Limitations of Implicit Testing	38
	How to Get Started with Implicit Testing	38
	When to Use Implicit Testing	39
	What's Next	39
6	**Evolving Neuromarketing 2.0 Tools**	**41**
	EEG Testing	41
	EEG Hardware Progress	42
	Virtual and Augmented Reality	42
	What's Next: From Insight to Influence	43

PART III   AI-POWERED PERSUASION   45

7	**Your AI Behavioral Science Dream Team**	**47**
	Your New Million-Dollar Team (That Costs Less Than Lunch)	48
	It's Not About the AI, It's About the Expert	49
	Generic Prompts Give Generic Results	50
	A Quick Caution on All-Knowing AI	51
	Building Your Dream Team	52
	Behavioral Science and Persuasion	52
	Customer Experience (CX) Experts	54
	Copywriting & Communication Experts	55
	Pricing Psychology & Strategy Experts	55
	Sales Experts	56
	Prompting Your Team	57
	Testing Your Team	58
	Single Expert vs. Multiple Experts	58
	Different Specific Experts for the Same Challenge	58

	Detailed Role vs. Specific Experts	59
	Different AI Models with the Same Expert Prompt	59
	Making Roles Work: Best Practices	59
	Put Your Team to Work	62
	What's Next	63
8	**Advanced Prompting**	**65**
	Frameworks Add Structure	66
	RACE (Role, Action, Context, Execute/Expectation)	66
	AIDA (Attention, Interest, Desire, Action)	66
	APE (Action, Purpose, Expectation)	66
	TAG (Task, Action, Goal)	67
	Six Rules of Thumb for Prompting AI Models	67
	Rule #1: Be Ridiculously Specific	67
	Rule #2: Give AI Everything at the Start	68
	Rule #3: Trust but Verify	68
	Rule #4: Save Your Best Prompts	68
	Rule #5: Introduce the Unexpected	69
	Rule #6: Kaizen Your AI	69
	Meta-Prompting: Let AI Build Better Prompts	69
	Share Your Knowledge: Add Context	71
	Start with Your Customers	72
	Customer Profile Framework	72
	Your Business and Your Brand	73
	The Industry and Competition	73
	Let AI Unlock Your Knowledge	74
	The Interview Approach	74
	Missing Context? AI Can Help	76
	The Gap-Filling Framework	76
	The Iteration Approach	77

Deep Research for Deep Insights	77
Create Your Customer Profiles	78
Researching Your Industry and Competitors	80
Reality Check	82
Learning from History	83
Reusing and Updating Your Knowledge	84
Projects and Custom GPTs	84
Update Frequently	86
Case Study: The Power of Iteration	87
Overnight Success? Nope	88
The Lesson: Iterate, Iterate, Iterate	89
Making It Work in Practice	89
The Multiplier Effect	90
Your First Mission	90
Your AI Changes You (in a Good Way)	91
A Quick Word About Ethics	92
Your Persuasion Control Center	92
What's Next	94
9 Quick Wins to Get Started	**95**
The Five-Minute Behavioral Audit	95
Go Deeper When It's Important	97
Get a Second Opinion	98
Score a Quick Win with a Better Headline	100
Headline Makeover: Loss Aversion in Action	101
Stack Your Triggers	102
Your Next Quick Win: Level Up Your CTA	102
Another Quick Win: Social Proof Power-Ups	105
Compound Your Quick Wins	108
Try It Out	108
What's Next	109

10 Attention and Emotion — 111

- Cognitive Overload — 111
- The Simplicity Paradox — 112
- Visual Complexity — 114
- Color Your World — 115
- Open the Curiosity Gap — 116
- Pattern Interruption to Get Attention — 117
- Emotional Triggers That Drive Results — 118
  - Pro Move #1: Build on What You've Learned — 120
  - Pro Move #2: Get More Powerful Insights with Deep Research — 120
- Emotional Copy Persuades — 122
- Keep Readers Moving Forward — 123
- The Attention-Emotion Feedback Loop — 124
- Your Attention Audit — 124
- What's Next — 125

11 Close the Credibility Gap — 127

- The Neuroscience of Trust — 128
- Digital Trust — 128
- Getting Started: A Trust Audit — 129
  - Use an Agent or Deep Research for a Thorough Trust Audit — 130
- The Social Proof Spectrum — 132
- Authority: The Expert Effect — 133
- Microcommitments to Build Trust — 134
- Anti-Trust Signals: Find Your Credibility Killers — 136
- Trust Transference Strategies — 137
  - Trust Transference Example — 138
  - Trust Transference Example with Deep Research — 138
- What's Next — 139

12 Decision Architecture and Pricing — 141
- The Choice Paradox in Practice — 141
  - Gemini on Gemini — 143
- The Decoy Effect: Steering Preference — 143
- Default Power: Frictionless Choice — 144
- Anchoring in Action — 145
  - Example: Pricing Page with Five Choices — 146
  - Example: Single Product — 146
- Loss Framing vs. Gain Framing — 147
- Temporal Framing: "When" Beats "What" — 148
- Choice Architecture and Pricing Psychology Audit — 149
- What's Next — 150

13 Scarcity, Urgency, and FOMO — 151
- The Psychology of Scarcity — 151
- Scarcity's Dark Side — 152
- Find Your Scarcity — 153
  - Example: Ad Agency — 153
  - Example—Luggage Brand — 154
- Authentic vs. Artificial Scarcity — 155
- Urgency Without Anxiety — 156
- The Scarcity Spectrum — 157
- Power Up Scarcity with Social Proof — 159
  - Ethical Scarcity — 160
- What's Next — 160

14 Advanced AI Behavioral Techniques — 161
- Multi-Expert Panels: Beyond Single Perspectives — 161
- Food Fight: Make Your Experts Disagree — 164
- Mobile-Specific Behavioral Psychology — 165
- B2B Behavioral Differences — 166

Fear as a B2B Motivator 167
Competitive Behavioral Analysis 168
Building Your Behavioral Prompt Library 171
Wrapping Up Part 3 172
What's Next 173

PART IV EMPATHY, EMOTION, AND COMMUNICATION 175

15 AI Adds the Human Touch 177
It's Humans That Lack Empathy 178
The High Cost of Lacking Empathy 178
Cruising Toward Disaster 179
Royal Caribbean's Great Adventure 180
    The Empathy Failure 181
    Loyalty, Shmoyalty 181
    Permanent Debarkation 182
AI Could Have Warned Them . . . 183
The Hidden Cost of Emotional Blindness 183
Closing the Empathy Gap 184
The Emotional Multiplier Effect 184
What AI "Empathy" Actually Means 185
Scientists Compare AI and Human Emotional Intelligence 186
What's Next 187

16 Auditing for Empathy 189
The 60-Second Emotion Check 189
    Step 1: Set the Context 189
    Step 2: Assess the Emotional Impact 190
    Step 3: Suggest Improvements 190
The Empathy Audit: Seeing Through Your Recipients' Eyes 191

The Empathy Audit Framework	192
The AI-Powered Empathy Check	193
Why Comprehensive Analysis Matters	194
The Power of Segment Analysis	196
Making It Actionable	196
What's Next	197
17 Practical Empathy	**199**
Customer-Facing Communications	199
Internal Communications	200
Crisis Communications	201
Personalized Emotional Intelligence	201
Segment-Specific Empathy	201
AI-Powered Emotional Personalization	202
Building Your AI Empathy System	203
Starter Prompts for Emotion and Empathy	203
Customer Reaction Predictor	204
Empathy Rewriter	204
Cultural Sensitivity Check	204
Stakeholder-Specific Communication	205
Give Your AI Feedback	205
Set Up Your Workflow	205
Don't Forget It's AI	206
The Future of Emotionally Intelligent Business	207
Predictive Emotional Intelligence	207
Cross-Cultural Emotional AI	208
Multimodal Empathy	208
Is Artificial Empathy Ethical?	208
Transparency and Authenticity	208
The Manipulation Question	209
The Empathy Advantage	209

Conclusion	211
Appendix: Classic Neuromarketing	213
Notes	233
Acknowledgments	239
About the Author	241
Index	243

Introduction

Your customers haven't changed in the last few years, but the tools to understand them, persuade them, and communicate with them *have* changed. And that's good news if your marketing budget and resources aren't unlimited.

Every marketer knows that their customers don't make decisions in a rational, analytical way. Gerald Zaltman of Harvard famously said that 95% of human thought processes are non-conscious. Long before that, common wisdom (sometimes attributed to sales legend Zig Ziglar) said, "Customers buy with emotion, and justify with logic."

So, as marketers, how do we understand what our customers *really* want? How do we know whether or not they'll buy what we're selling? And how do we create marketing that appeals to how their brains actually work?

Neuromarketing has been one answer. We can measure how our customers respond to our ads, packaging, pricing, etc., at a non-conscious level using tools like EEG brain wave measurement, biometrics, implicit testing, and more. And we can use the tools of behavioral science research to craft compelling messaging.

The problem is that historically these approaches have been expensive and time-consuming.

Big organizations could run lab studies and staff nudge units with behavioral science experts. Even in these large firms, very few marketing questions justified the time or expense required to use these resources.

For smaller companies and nonprofits, none of these tools were practical. At best, their marketers could read books on influence, persuasion, and consumer psychology, and then try to apply the ideas to their marketing.

That was then, this is now.

Today, inexpensive neuromarketing tools that don't require lab studies are multiplying. Artificial intelligence (AI) is partially eliminating the need for human subjects. Generative AI is bringing world-class behavior, persuasion, and emotional communication expertise to your desktop.

This book shows you how to use these tools to improve your marketing in ways that didn't exist a few years ago. Regardless of the size of your organization, you'll find new ways to understand your customers and create impactful marketing.

Welcome to Neuromarketing 2.0!

Part I

The Future of Marketing Is Here

"The trouble with market research is that people don't think how they feel, they don't say what they think and they don't do what they say."

—David Lewis, Neuropsychologist and Neuromarketing Pioneer

Chapter 1

A Short History of Neuromarketing

If you've ever watched a perfectly tested ad fall flat, or seen a product bomb despite positive focus group feedback, you've probably asked the same question many marketers do: What went wrong? The answer usually lies beneath the surface... the surface of your customer's mind.

Why Neuromarketing Is Important

Most human decisions aren't made with careful, conscious thought. Researcher Jonathan Haidt uses the metaphor of the elephant and rider to represent emotion and logic in decision-making. He says, "The mind is divided, like a rider on an elephant, and the rider's job is to serve the elephant."[1] Haidt says that the elephant decides, and the rider is left to explain the decision.

If customer decisions are heavily influenced by factors they aren't consciously aware of, there are big implications for three areas:

> **Customer Insights:** We can't merely ask customers questions and get answers that are accurate enough to support important decisions. We can ask what they like about a product, which design they prefer, or whether they will buy a product. That's how most market research is done even today. But those answers often aren't reliable. Sometimes, they are flat out wrong.

Persuading Customers: Even today, many marketing pitches are based on rational appeals: product features, benefits, competitive comparisons, and so on. This isn't necessarily bad, but logical arguments are rarely enough to convince the customer to act. Selectively employing non-conscious appeals based on behavioral science, like social proof, scarcity, anchoring, priming, and dozens of others, can dramatically improve results.

Connecting and Communicating Emotionally: Businesses are constantly communicating with their customers. Major policy announcements, routine order messages, and call center conversations are all part of the process. Far too often, these communications are transactional, devoid of emotion or empathy. Sometimes, this lack of empathy or emotional intelligence leads to customer anger or frustration. To build an emotional connection with its customers and to be sure that messaging lands as expected, every organization needs to talk to its customers in a way that incorporates emotional intelligence and empathy.

■ ■ ■

Understanding our customers' brains helps us with every aspect of marketing. We can use neuromarketing insights to learn what customers really want. This knowledge can help us develop better products. We can create ads and marketing that perform better. We communicate in a way that builds connection with the brand.

Most importantly, we can avoid wasting money by identifying marketing that isn't going to move the needle. "Half the money I spend on advertising is wasted, the trouble is I don't know which half," is a quote attributed to department store magnate John Wanamaker. The true amount of wasted marketing spend is likely even worse. Neuromarketing studies can identify the clunkers before they land with a thud and exhaust your budget but produce no results.

Even without hooking people up to EEG machines, we can make our marketing more persuasive by using messaging aimed at the way people's brains work. Behavior science, consumer psychology, behavioral economics, and related fields of research are a goldmine for marketers trying to be more effective.

Neuroscience and Marketing?

In the early 2000s, two disparate fields, neuroscience and marketing, were coming together. People were talking about a new field, "neuromarketing." fMRI studies purported to show which Super Bowl ads worked best. Big brands began using a variety of techniques to evaluate non-conscious reactions to their brands, advertising, and products.

These early years weren't without controversy. Some early neuromarketing service providers were making claims that didn't seem to be well-supported. The link between measured changes in brain activity and real-world sales was often tenuous. Eminent neuroscience researchers called the entire concept of neuromarketing into question, at least in terms of the conclusions being reached by some of the field's proponents.[2] Even when neuromarketing research was solid, it was so expensive that only the biggest brands could afford it.

Personally, I gravitated more to the other aspect of neuromarketing: taking the work of neuroscientists, behavioral scientists, consumer psychologists, and others and showing how to apply this science to marketing *without* expensive studies. This affordable, nearly free, approach appealed to many marketers. Unlike costly neuromarketing research, these techniques could be used by anyone at little or no cost.

Neuromarketing Through the Years

What I call "classic neuromarketing" has evolved into an increasingly respected discipline. Many big brands employ it. Universities, mostly in

Europe, today offer degrees in neuromarketing. Various studies peg the annual global spending on neuromarketing at well over a billion dollars,[3] hardly a fringe movement.

Classic neuromarketing studies are done primarily in lab settings: academic research facilities, service providers, and in house laboratories. Techniques include fMRI, EEG, eye tracking, facial coding, biometrics, and more. These lab studies are useful and important, but aren't usually practical for answering the vast majority of marketing questions, even in big organizations. The Appendix describes the lab-based techniques available to marketers today.

Behavioral Science for All

Behavioral science tools have become universally accepted by marketers. Big companies have behavioral science teams, sometimes called nudge units, to improve marketing and encourage positive behaviors by employees. Conversion optimization experts have studied social science research and influence psychology to find ways to convert more website visitors and increase sales.

Sophisticated marketers like those in the travel industry make extensive use of science-based triggers. "Only two rooms left! 53 people booked this hotel today!" uses scarcity and social proof, two well-established influence principles.

Even small companies that haven't studied the underlying science know that using testimonials and a crossed-out high price next to the actual price can boost sales.

The Pandemic Push

COVID-19 disrupted practically everything, and neuromarketing service providers felt the impact quickly. Recruiting subjects and bringing them into a laboratory to get wired up and watch ads became nearly impossible. The largest provider of services globally before the pandemic hit was Nielsen Neuroscience. They closed their labs and fired most of their neuroscientists.[4]

If there was anything good about this stressful time it's that neuromarketing tools that could be used remotely got a huge boost. Fringe ideas like eye tracking and reading facial expressions with phone cameras and webcams became far more interesting. During and even after the pandemic, companies accelerated efforts to develop tools that would work outside the laboratory, including concepts like smartwatch-based biometric measurements.

The AI Transformation

Even before the pandemic, artificial intelligence was beginning to have an impact. Machine learning AI models trained on thousands of human eye-tracking studies could predict with reasonable accuracy where human subjects would look.

More recent advances in generative AI tools like ChatGPT and Claude have, among other things, opened up behavioral science marketing to everyone. Today you don't need a degree in consumer psychology, and you don't need to read dozens of books. Properly prompted, these LLMs can become your personal nudge unit, showing you how to apply the ideas of brilliant researchers to your marketing messaging.

Personally, I've changed much of my writing and teaching to focus less on explaining the ideas of thinkers like Robert Cialdini and Daniel Kahneman and more on showing how AI can help apply their ideas and those of many other smart people.

Neuromarketing 2.0

These two developments—inexpensive tools and on-demand AI expertise—create a fundamentally different kind of neuromarketing. Small agencies, nonprofits, startups, and even solopreneurs can now employ techniques that used to be just for big brands.

Even in large companies, these new low-cost approaches mean that neuromarketing can be used to answer a vast number of questions previously out of reach. Nobody would have spent thousands of dollars to test alternate layouts for an individual page on a website. Today, a web designer can do just that in minutes, for the price of a cup of coffee.

These developments are incredibly exciting. When I began writing about neuromarketing, many of the topics I covered couldn't be used by most of my readers. Neuromarketing was too expensive, too complicated, or required an impractical amount of effort.

Today, it's different. Neuroscience, marketing, behavioral science, and artificial intelligence have come together to form a discipline that is simultaneously more powerful and more affordable.

It's so different that it justifies its own name, Neuromarketing 2.0.

In the chapters that follow, we'll begin to explore how elite consumer neuroscience tools have been democratized.

For updates and copy/paste prompt text visit rogerdooley.com/engine.

Part II

The New Tools of Neuromarketing

On-Demand Insights

The huge change in the neuromarketing space is a shift from a focus on expensive lab studies to using tools that are available on-demand and at modest cost. Most of the tools we'll discuss are available as SaaS models—software as a service. Most have monthly subscription fees that are affordable for smaller companies, agencies, and nonprofits.

This flips the script for marketers. Instead of having to figure out how to justify an expensive lab study, the challenge now is finding new ways to use neuromarketing to answer ever smaller but important questions.

Chapter 2

Eye-Tracking Revolution

Eye tracking is one of the most straightforward and useful tools to measure actual customer behavior. Eye-tracking studies use sensors, special glasses, or cameras to record where subjects look when viewing something. A few questions the technique can answer for print ads, websites, and videos include:

1. What do people see first? Second? Third?
2. What do people almost never see?
3. Do browsing users easily see the "buy" button or other call to action?
4. How much attention, if any, does the brand logo get?
5. What holds people's attention the longest?

Eye-tracking data can be used to produce heat maps, not unlike a weather forecaster's thunderstorm map. Intense color shows what people looked at most. Opacity maps black out the image and show only those areas that were viewed. Gaze paths show the order of things that people viewed.

Different layouts can be compared to see which produces the most attention where the marketer wants it. If the first web page test shows that few people spotted the "Request More Information" call to action, you can make the button bigger, move it higher, and change its color. A retest will show how effective that is. You can repeat as necessary.

Even by itself, eye tracking can be very useful. In combination with other neuromarketing tools, it can show what produced the measured human responses, i.e., what the subject was viewing while they showed a change in brain or biometric activity.

Which Book Cover Gets Attention?

Let's look at a real-world example to see the value of eye tracking and its evolution over time.

My fellow Austinite, best-selling author and podcaster Tim Ferriss, tested his early book covers by printing mock-ups of different cover designs. He put these covers on physical books and placed them on a table in a bookstore like Barnes & Noble. He then watched from an inconspicuous spot to see which of the variations was picked up most often by shoppers. Do this multiple times in different stores, and you'll get a good idea of which cover option is most likely to be picked up, a necessary precursor to actual sale.

Ferriss's approach was a quick and cost-effective way to test cover designs to maximize bookstore sales.

My Experiment: Book Covers in Online Stores

In the months before my book *Friction* released, my publisher sent me the cover design. It was a sort of pale yellow, and I didn't think it would stand out on an e-commerce site. By this time, bookstores were struggling, and the vast majority of books were sold on Amazon or other websites. Most commonly, I assumed, people would see a thumbnail image of the cover in search results or lists of suggested titles. Testing cover variations using physical books on a bookstore table might produce results that didn't translate to e-commerce.

I should point out that a book cover decision for authors other than Stephen King or James Clear doesn't warrant much effort or expense. For most business books from non-famous authors, the publisher designs a cover and sends it to the author for a perfunctory check. Sometimes authors push back and get major revisions, but the publisher is the final decision-maker.

So, how could I get my publisher to change the yellow cover? I mocked up a few different versions of the cover in different colors. I was attending a neuromarketing conference and showed the cover variations to some of my smart colleagues to get their opinion on the publisher's version and my variations. One volunteered, "Why don't we do an eye tracking test?"

To be clear, a book cover decision would not normally justify an eye-tracking test using costly sensor-laden glasses, recruited subjects, and lab technician time. But since my friend was kind enough to offer the service, I mocked up four thumbnail lineups with the publisher's cover and three other versions with different color combinations. Each lineup had four randomly chosen business books, two on each side and mine in the middle.

A better study would have randomized the position and the other book cover designs/colors. Position in a row matters, as does the appearance of the other targets. I didn't want to abuse my friend's generosity, so we just tested the four basic lineups.

The findings were clear: when presented in a row of Amazon-style thumbnails, a black cover design drew far more attention than the yellow cover and my other color options. (A dark blue cover did fairly well, too.) When I shared the study data with the publisher, they agreed to go with the black version.

It's important to note that this tested only which color was more "visually salient," i.e., more likely to attract the gaze of viewers. It didn't show which variant would get more clicks, or which would sell better online. It certainly didn't predict how well the cover would perform in bookstores. But getting the customer's attention is the first step to an online sale.

Equally important is that I never would have been able to justify the cost of a full lab eye-tracking study for the cover of a wonky business book with zero chance of hitting the *New York Times* bestseller list, great cover or not.

Can Less Expensive, Faster Techniques Work?

Lots of business decisions are like that book cover: you'd like to make an informed decision, but the amount of revenue involved doesn't justify spending thousands of dollars for one data point. Eye tracking can tell you what customers will see and/or look at, but not much else. If you have little or no budget, perhaps any market research efforts should focus more on understanding what customers will buy.

Business decisions like redesigning a package for a low-volume product, creating an ad for a trade publication, choosing an image for a product page on your website, picking the backdrop for your conference display, etc., all fall into that category. In most cases, the designer makes a choice. The boss approves it or suggests a change. End of story.

The good news is that vastly cheaper and faster substitutes for lab-based eye tracking exist today.

The Experiment Continues: Device Camera Eye Tracking

What if instead of bringing people into a lab to view your content, you could use cameras that everyone already has in their home or office? Webcams, phone cameras, etc.?

In fact, this technology exists today as a software service. For a keynote at a big marketing conference in Milan, Italy, I replicated my original experiment with the book cover thumbnails. By using the software company's subjects for my panel, in less than a day I had eye-tracking results with a sample size of 35. (I could have recruited my own subjects, but that would have taken longer.)

The heat maps generated were not nearly as well-defined as those from lab eye tracking. The hot spots were blobby and diffused. Looking at the heat map alone, I would have been hard pressed to pick a winner.

Fortunately, there was a wealth of quantitative data behind the heat maps. Examining that, I found the black cover was the leader in all the important metrics—views, gazes, gaze duration, and repeat views. Despite the messy heat map, the webcam/device cam experiment produced the same winner.

Who Needs Humans?

Artificial intelligence has exploded in recent years with the advent of powerful generative AI and large language models like ChatGPT and Claude. But long before generative AI emerged as a powerful tool, machine learning was being used in a variety of applications.

In the early years of AI, there were "expert systems"—human experts described how they did their work, and coders turned this knowledge into a rules-based process that could be accessed by an end user or a less-skilled support person. This worked well in some situations, but poorly in others. As a human, you can no doubt identify a pictured animal as a cat with 100% accuracy in milliseconds. But creating a rules-based process for identifying specific animals would be next to impossible.

Machine learning creates algorithms by training. Give the software enough pictures of cats and even more pictures of non-cats (dogs, monkeys, cars, etc.) and it will eventually get good at identifying the felines.

It turns out this process works with eye tracking. Train an algorithm on the results of thousands of human eye-tracking studies, and it can get very good at predicting where people will look on a new image or video.

Repeating the Book Experiment with AI Eye-Tracking Simulators

I repeated the book cover thumbnail experiment with three different AI eye-tracking simulators. I was surprised at how different the heat maps were from each other and also from the original lab study. One had horizontal bands that ran across the images and text. Another had big, round hot spots on all the covers, with the covers closest to the center being the "hottest." A third produced heat maps closer to the original lab study, albeit a bit more diffused.

The good news? Comparing the heat maps and quantitative data for the different covers, all three AI models picked the same winner as the lab study.

The companies that offer these eye-tracking simulators claim 90–95% accuracy, sometimes higher. Looking at the wide variation in predictions for the three models, one would immediately question those claims. Why would the three models produce such different heat maps?

The answer, I think, lies in the training data. It's unlikely that there were many (or any) training images that looked like my cover thumbnail lineups. So, the algorithms had to extrapolate from their knowledge of other images.

I recall seeing an AI-generated heat map for an image of an attractive woman in a bikini. The model's face was the main hot spot, with the rest of her getting little attention. A human face in an image is almost always the first thing people look at, so the AI wasn't far off. But lab studies show that both men and women will look at the rest of a scantily-clad human body, too.[1] Predictably, perhaps, one human eye-tracking experiment with an unclad (but strategically covered) female model wearing Reeboks showed male viewers barely saw her shoes![2]

If you trained an AI model with human eye-tracking data for rows of book covers or ads featuring swimsuit models, it would no doubt get quite accurate at predicting how new images in those categories would be viewed.

Book Experiment Takeaway

My little experiments show both the limitations and power of low-cost eye-tracking methods. None of the heat maps—webcam or AI simulation—closely duplicated the lab test results. But, in each case they picked the same cover as being the most visually salient.

The AI tools should perform better in common scenarios like a print ad or web page since they are likely to have trained on many similar images. And the AI tools will keep getting better as they are trained on more lab study results.

Remote Eye Tracking

Wouldn't it be great if you could conduct eye-tracking experiments outside of a laboratory and without expensive glasses or sensors? Maybe even using your actual customers instead of stand-ins? The good news is that today you can. The only bad news is that the resolution isn't as good as a professional lab setup. That's what I found in my book experiment.

As you'll see throughout this book, the tradeoff is "good vs. good enough." If you're working on a home page redesign for your eight-figure e-commerce website or a package redesign affecting dozens of products that need to stand out on supermarket shelves, you should probably look for the best eye-tracking data available.

At the other end of the spectrum, perhaps you've got projects like a one-off print ad for a specialty magazine. Or you need to choose between a dozen possible banner ad designs. For comparatively low-value efforts like these, even less precise eye-tracking data can improve your decisions.

Limitations of Remote Eye Tracking

Webcam and phone-based eye tracking can be a useful and affordable way to find out what people look at when they view ads, websites, or product designs. But there are some clear limits. These tools aren't as accurate as special lab equipment. A webcam can tell you what part of a screen someone is looking at, like a headline or image, but it can't pinpoint exact words or small details. Lighting, camera quality, and how still someone sits also affect how well the tracking works.

Another challenge is timing. Webcams usually record fewer images per second than lab tools, so they can miss quick eye movements or very short glances. Also, if a person moves their head too much or doesn't follow the setup steps properly, the collected data might be wrong. That's why researchers often need more subjects in webcam studies to make sure the results are reliable. Of course, scaling the sample size with remote participants and no special equipment is much easier and cheaper than scaling a lab study.

Overall, webcam eye tracking is useful for fast, simple studies, but not ideal when you need very precise or detailed data.

How to Use Remote Eye Tracking

Getting started with webcam or phone-based eye tracking is surprisingly easy, even for a small business or ad agency without a big research budget. The first step is to choose a platform that offers remote eye-tracking tools designed for non-experts. Services like RealEye, Sticky by

Tobii, CoolTool, and EyeSee all let you upload visuals and run tests with real people using just their webcams or phone cameras. These images could include things like a print ad, website, or packaging mockup.

The platforms handle the technical setup, guiding participants through calibration and capturing their gaze data automatically. You'll get clear outputs like heat maps, gaze trails, and simple metrics showing what people looked at and for how long.

You can start small: test one design with 30–50 participants to get a basic sense of what grabs attention and what's being missed. Most platforms offer built-in recruiting options, or you can send your test link to your own panel, social followers, or email list. Some even offer free trial credits or low-cost pay-per-test pricing, so you don't need a subscription to try out the service.

To get the most value, plan your test to answer specific questions. For example: "Do people notice our brand logo quickly?" or "Are they reading the headline before looking at the product?" After running a study, most platforms provide visual reports that make it easy to explain findings to clients or your team. Over time, you can use these tools to compare creative ideas, improve ad effectiveness, and show clients how their designs perform in the real world.

If you're also curious about how viewers *feel* about your content, product, etc., look for platforms that include facial expression analysis alongside gaze tracking—this lets you see both what people look at and how they react emotionally. We'll cover that option in the next chapter.

AI Eye-Tracking Simulators

What's one thing that would be on any market researcher's wish list? One would be the ability to conduct research without human subjects.

Recruiting people for studies, focus groups, etc., is time-consuming and expensive. There's the constant danger of selecting a sample that poorly represents potential customers. Eye-tracking simulators are one solution.

Because there's a wealth of human eye-tracking data, machine learning AI can develop algorithms that do a reasonable job of predicting where real humans will look. And, since the whole process has been compressed into a piece of software, studies can be not only cheaply but quickly.

While not a perfect substitute for human eye-tracking studies, AI simulators can be used for many applications that couldn't justify their time and expense of using human subjects.

How to Use AI Eye-Tracking Simulators

AI simulators are a great tool when marketing budgets are limited. Small businesses, boutique agencies, and even smaller business units in large enterprises often end up making creative choices without the benefit of pretesting options. With AI eye tracking, they can get quick, affordable insights. Here are a few examples:

- A local coffee shop designing a flyer for a new drink special could upload the design and see if people will actually notice the price or the call to action.
- An Etsy seller could test different versions of a product photo or label design to see which one grabs more attention.
- A new online store could check if visitors will notice the "Add to Cart" button on product pages right away.
- When designing a billboard, an agency can make sure the brand name or main message is easy to spot.
- An agency can compare two ad concepts and choose the one more likely to catch the customer's eye.

Even larger businesses can take advantage of AI eye-tracking's speed and affordability. For example, they can:

- Test dozens of ad or package designs and quickly rule out weak ones.
- Check if a product's new label is easy to spot on a crowded supermarket shelf.
- Make sure customers focus on the most important parts of an email, webpage, or mobile app.

Some companies now use these tools as part of their regular design process. It saves time, cuts costs, and helps them avoid mistakes that could hurt sales.

Pros and Cons of AI Eye Tracking

Why do I like AI eye tracking? Not because it's perfect, but because it provides data that is usually much better than nothing.

Data vs. Guessing

In most cases, the alternative to AI eye tracking isn't expensive lab studies. It's guesswork. A designer makes the decisions or perhaps comes up with a few alternatives. Then, the team tries to reach a consensus as to which will perform best. Or the boss decides.

AI eye tracking helps designers prove their designs work. Instead of saying "this looks good," they can show clients or their boss a heat map and gaze path that say, "here's what customers will see first." It's a bit like having a visual design expert sitting in the meeting. This expert might not understand the product, the brand, or the messaging but can still provide advice about what customers will look at in typical situations.

A Big Caution

As much as I like AI eye tracking, I would never trust it completely. As fast and useful as these tools are, they aren't perfect. They predict where people are likely to look based on patterns from past eye-tracking studies. But they don't know *why* someone is looking or what they're *thinking*. For example, a heat map might show that people will notice a big red banner, but it can't tell if they read the text or just glanced at the color. AI simulators also don't account for real-world factors like a person's goals, emotions, or cultural background, all of which can influence what someone pays attention to.

Another key point: these tools are best at predicting first glances, not deeper engagement. They won't tell you how customers are going to digest your text bullets or paragraphs of copy. They're great for spotting design problems early, but they don't replace real lab studies or feedback from actual customers.

The last caution is that just like human eye tracking, AI simulators only predict attention. They can show that website visitors will *see* your call to action, but not whether they will actually click it or take any other action.

The Power of Fast Iteration

What sets AI eye tracking apart from other ways of evaluating visual content is its speed. In a matter of minutes, you can try different versions of a design—change the layout, colors, or image placement—and see how each one performs. I find a simple design tool like Canva, Adobe Express, or Snappa handy for iterating quickly. For example, rather than editing a live web page to test variations, just use a screenshot and an image editing tool to make the headline bigger, swap an image, change the CTA color, etc.

I'm no graphic designer, but I used the free version of Canva to try multiple variations on my own website's home page call to action.

I started with a screen capture of the visible part of the home page and ran it through Feng-GUI. The original CTA, a small blue link, was mostly invisible, according to the AI. I kept increasing the font size and adding color until it became likely to attract sufficient attention. The whole process, including four design variations, took barely 30 minutes.

How to Get Started with AI Eye Tracking

Getting started with AI eye tracking is simple and doesn't require any special equipment or training. All you need is a digital image of what you want to test. This could be a product package, a social media ad, a flyer, a webpage, or even a shelf display mockup.

You'll need to sign up with an AI eye-tracking platform like Feng-GUI, Attention Insight, EyeQuant, Neurons Inc.'s Predict or Expoze.io. Many offer free trials or pay-as-you-go plans, so you don't need a big budget to experiment. You upload your image and make a few choices to set the image's context and help the model analyze it. A web page and an outdoor billboard don't get viewed in the same way by real humans, and most models take differences like this into account.

Within seconds, you'll get a heat map showing which areas are most likely to attract attention during the first few seconds of viewing. Some tools offer opacity maps, with all of the image blacked out except for the areas predicted to get attention. Gaze paths, an indication of what people will see first, second, etc., are common. Some give you scores, rankings, and other quantitative data to help you evaluate how visible your logo or call to action is.

For any marketer with a limited budget (that's just about every marketer, right?), AI eye tracking is a fast and affordable way to test and improve marketing materials before spending serious money on printing, advertising, or development. Start by testing your most important visuals (like your homepage or product label) and use what you learn to guide your creative decisions. It's a quick way to make smarter design choices and increase the chances that customers notice what matters most.

What's Next

Eye-tracking data tells you what people see, but not how they react. That's why it's often used in conjunction with other techniques that gauge emotion or arousal. Knowing what subjects are looking at when changes are seen helps interpret the results.

In the next chapter, we'll look at facial coding—analyzing changes in expression to track emotion. Some services offer both eye tracking and facial coding using the same software and device camera, making it a simple enhancement that helps marketers understand customer reactions.

For updates and copy/paste prompt text visit rogerdooley.com/engine.

Chapter 3

Facial Coding

For decades, scientists have used facial coding, or facial expression analysis, to tease out the emotions a person is experiencing. Dr. Paul Ekman, the pioneer in the field, developed his facial action coding system (FACS) designed to categorize every human facial expression and relate those to the underlying emotions. (See the Appendix for more details.)

Traditionally, facial coding experiments were done by expert "coders" reviewing slow-motion video of subjects' faces. Slowing down the video enabled the coders to catch "microexpressions," fleeting expressions believed to reflect the subject's true emotion before they consciously or unconsciously adopted a socially acceptable expression.

The need for expert review of recorded sessions made facial coding relatively slow and expensive.

Remote, Real-Time Facial Coding

Two technologies have made facial coding less costly and easier to scale. First, as with eye tracking, the continued improvement of webcams and phone cameras makes using them practical for facial coding. These device cameras track small movements in the face—like a smile, frown, raised eyebrows, or a furrowed brow. These movements are then matched to common emotional reactions, such as happiness, surprise, anger, or confusion.

Second, AI software algorithms developed by machine learning are capable of replacing the human experts. Not only that, they are fast enough to work in real time. The software does this automatically, without the need for a person to watch the video.

Marketers and researchers use facial coding to see how people react to things like ads, product packaging, websites, or videos. For example, if someone smiles while watching a commercial, that's a sign they liked it. If their expression shows surprise or confusion, it might mean that something in the message wasn't clear. Because this happens while the person is watching—without asking them any questions—it helps capture honest reactions that they might not say out loud or even be able to express.

Limitations of Device Camera Facial Coding

All forms of facial coding have limits. It's not always 100% accurate. Not everyone shows emotions the same way. Some people hide what they feel, or their culture teaches them to keep a straight face. And just because someone shows a certain expression doesn't always mean they feel that emotion deeply. It could just be a quick response to something surprising or odd.

Using webcams and phone cameras with automated software analysis adds another layer of difficulty. The software can usually recognize clear expressions like happiness or surprise very well, but it may struggle with more subtle emotions or fleeting microexpressions.

The first time I tried one of these tools on myself, I watched a short cartoon. It was moderately amusing, but when I looked at the emotions I exhibited, you wouldn't have guessed that. In fact, you might have thought I slept through the whole thing. My resting grumpy face barely changed, and the emotion graph was a nearly flat line. The technology has improved since then, but this highlights individual differences in reactions and expressiveness.

Even with these limitations, facial coding can be a helpful tool. When combined with other methods like eye tracking or surveys, it can give a fuller picture of how people respond to what they see.

How to Use Facial Coding

Getting started with facial coding is much easier today than when it required watching slow-motion recordings. Many platforms that offer webcam-based eye tracking, like CoolTool, RealEye, Synapbox, Noldus, and EyeSee, also include facial coding as part of their service.

These platforms use the participant's webcam or phone camera to detect facial expressions while they look at an ad, website, or product image. You don't need any special equipment or technical knowledge. The platform handles the video analysis and gives you clear results, like charts showing when people smiled, looked confused, or reacted emotionally.

To begin, choose a platform and create an account. Unfortunately, these tools don't currently have an option to easily subscribe using a monthly SaaS model.

If you find a platform that fits your budget, you'll upload the content you want to test, like a video ad or product packaging mockup, and set up a few questions if you want feedback. Then, you send a link to participants. Some platforms can help you recruit people, or you can use your own email list or social media followers. As participants watch your content, the software tracks their facial expressions in real time and shows you when and how they reacted emotionally.

If eye-tracking data is being recorded, you'll also be able to match emotional peaks and transitions to what people were looking at.

Once the test is done, you'll get an easy-to-understand report. It might show that most viewers smiled at the funny part of your ad, or that they looked puzzled when your call to action appeared. You can use these insights to improve your messaging, design, or timing.

Facial coding won't tell you everything, but it gives you feedback on emotion that eye tracking alone can't provide and that surveys often miss. It's a fast, reasonably affordable way for small teams to add emotional intelligence to their creative process. Most importantly, it can help your work connect more deeply with the people you're trying to reach.

What's Next

Your test subjects may have some control over the expressions they exhibit on their faces, but almost nobody can control variables like their heartbeat, body temperature, palm perspiration, etc. In the next chapter, we'll see the progress in taking biometric measurements out of the laboratory using wearable and mobile technology.

For updates and copy/paste prompt text visit rogerdooley.com/engine.

Chapter 4

Biometrics Everywhere

If we want to measure how people unconsciously respond to something—an ad, a product, a video, etc.—biometric measurements are a solid alternative to more complicated and expensive brain scanning or brain wave measurement. Common biometric measurements include galvanic skin response, heart rate, heart rate variability, breathing rate, body temperature, and more.

Innerscope Research, later acquired by Nielsen Neuroscience, was an early provider of neuromarketing services that used biometrics for its studies. Its founder, Dr. Carl Marci, once commented that they didn't include EEG testing as part of their measurement suite because the limited additional data it provided didn't justify the expense. Biometric measurements alone were sufficient, he said.

In the past, biometric studies meant bringing subjects into a lab and wiring them up with various sensors—heart rate, breathing, galvanic skin response, and more. The data collected would then have to be interpreted and turned into a report on how subjects reacted to what they were seeing or experiencing. The results were reliable, but the process was comparatively expensive.

The Wearable Revolution

Today, wearables smartwatches and fitness trackers can do things that used to require complicated equipment and dedicated spaces. They can perform an electrocardiogram. They can measure your breathing rate and blood oxygen. Not only do they know when you are asleep, they can determine what stage of sleep you are in. They can measure skin temperature and physical activity. Even complex measurements like blood pressure and blood glucose levels are within reach.

Given that, it's no surprise that neuromarketers are turning to wearables as the next frontier in customer insights. Combine a smartwatch and a smartphone app, and you've got the ingredients for an inexpensive, highly mobile biometric monitor.

The Advantages of Wearables

The advantages of using wearables for neuromarketing studies are obvious.

It's cheaper. Lots of people already have the equipment and only need to install an app. Even if a marketer wants to provide the gear for simplicity or consistency purposes, inexpensive smartphones and wearables are readily available.

It's portable. Studies can be done anywhere. Subjects can sit and watch a screen, but they can also walk around. They can be engaged in some kind of experience, like a training workshop or visit to a retail store. They can experience just about anything in the same way a "normal," unmonitored person would.

It's minimally intrusive. Unlike, say, portable EEG headsets, smartwatches are unobtrusive and part of daily life. Subjects quickly forget they are being monitored as they engage with content or an experience.

Barriers to Wearables

If there's one thing preventing widespread adoption of wearables as neuromarketing tools is that the technology is new and changing quickly. Unlike EEG, wearables don't have years of accumulated data and published research that shows how to interpret results. A startup that wants to create an algorithm to turn biometric data into marketing insights would have to first do the primary research—an arduous and expensive process.

Some subjects may object to installing software on their personal devices. The workaround is for the experimenter to provide standardized devices preloaded with the software.

Immersion Neuroscience: Real-World Biometrics Made Simple

One company has cracked the wearable code.

Immersion Neuroscience has taken the kind of sophisticated neurophysiological measurement that used to require lab equipment and turned it into software that works with ordinary smartwatches and fitness bands. No gel in your hair. No wires. No lab.

From DARPA Labs to Your Wrist

A few years ago, I challenged Immersion founder Dr. Paul Zak by asking, "If my smartwatch can't even tell if I'm sleeping or awake, how can it measure what you call 'immersion?'" I related my experience with what was then a state-of-the-art smartwatch that would mistakenly log me as sleeping when I was working on my laptop or even playing video games. (I should note that in the ensuing years software updates eliminated that problem.)

Zak explained that the technology behind Immersion emerged from more than 15 years of Defense Advanced Research Projects Agency (DARPA) research aimed at understanding how messages and experiences influence behavior. He and his team spent nearly two decades measuring brain activity to predict emotional reactions. His team started by measuring neurochemicals like oxytocin, the "trust hormone," to understand how the brain values experiences.

The breakthrough happened when they found they could infer these neural states by analyzing heart activity measured at the wrist. Through sophisticated algorithms applied to cardiac rhythms, they created a single metric called "Immersion" that captures attention and emotional resonance.

What Can You Measure?

Immersion is intended to be a measure of how much someone's brain values an experience. When people are really engaged, both paying attention AND feeling an emotional connection, their Immersion scores rise.

Here are a few applications:

- **Retail Environments:** One study found that sales associates' peak Immersion levels predicted customer purchases with 64–80% accuracy in luxury retail settings.[1] When both the associate and customer showed high Immersion, sales followed. This matches up with an article I wrote years earlier explaining how hiring people passionate about the brand or product could increase sales.[2]
- **Content Testing:** The platform correctly identified which videos would go viral, which new songs would become hits, and which TV shows would top the ratings. It even predicted which ads would produce the largest sales bumps for five out of six brands in a controlled study.[3]
- **Training and Communications:** Companies like Accenture use Immersion to ensure employees are actually benefiting from training programs, not just sitting through them.[4]
- **Live Experiences:** Want to know if your conference presentation is landing? Or if that product demo is truly engaging customers? Immersion can measure it in real time.

How to Get Started

Measuring Immersion is designed to be accessible, hence the firm's tagline, "democratized neuroscience."

The setup is surprisingly straightforward:

- **Signup:** Free and paid monthly subscriptions are available at Known.cx. Usage fees based on data collection apply.
- **Equipment:** Participants wear a standard fitness band or smartwatch. No special hardware is required. If you plan to run frequent tests, investing in a set of standard bands and having participants wear them can simplify the process.
- **Software:** The Immersion mobile app, available for both Apple and Android phones, pairs with the wearable via Bluetooth. Companion apps are available for the wearable. Data streams to cloud servers in real time. As an alternative to having the app installed on each individual's smartphone, a Bluetooth hub can centralize data collection.
- **Analysis:** The platform provides cleaned, processed data showing when Immersion peaked, where it dropped, and what percentage of your audience was engaged at any moment.

The appeal to organizations with limited budgets is that you're not getting raw biometric data that requires an expert to interpret. Rather, you're getting intuitive metrics that answer practical questions: Did they care? When did we lose them? What moments created the strongest connection?

Sample applications could include:

- Testing two versions of a video ad to see which version created more emotional engagement.

- A retailer training sales staff to measure which approaches create genuine connections with customers.
- A nonprofit testing different stories and messages to see which ones create the emotional response most likely to inspire donations.

Limitations of Immersion

Immersion measures emotional engagement, not purchase intent (for marketing tests) or actual learning (evaluating training). It doesn't measure emotional valence, i.e., whether subjects were engaged because they loved or hated what they saw.

Privacy is another consideration. The app collects health and fitness data, which some participants might find intrusive. Typical use requires installing an app on the subject's phone, problematic for some people. (Some organizations provide standardized devices to test subjects to avoid this issue.)

And while the technology is more accessible than traditional neuromarketing tools, it's not free. You'll need to factor in the cost of the platform access and potentially the wearables if you're providing them.

Pairing Immersion with Other Methods

While Immersion can be used as a standalone approach, it can also be used in conjunction with other technologies. For example, eye-tracking data would tell you what people were looking at during periods of high or low engagement. Facial coding data would clarify what emotions were causing high levels of immersion.

What I find most compelling about Immersion is its combination of modest cost to try out and uncomplicated data presentation. For years, we've known that emotional engagement drives behavior. Now, you can measure it even with a modest marketing budget.

If you're curious, start small. Test it on your next important presentation or customer interaction. Compare what the data tells you with what you thought happened. You might be surprised by what you learn about when your audience truly connects—and when they're just being polite.

An even simpler way to see the technology in action is to try the company's consumer app, Six. It's meant to measure your own immersion throughout the day so you can identify those activities and behaviors that your brain finds most engaging. There's a fee to subscribe but you can test it for free. The purpose of the app is different, but the technology is the same as used in the commercial research version.

What's Next

Biometrics are a proven way to gauge reactions, but what about determining the hidden feelings and biases of your customers? Do they see your brand as innovative or behind the times? Exciting or boring? In the next chapter we'll look at implicit testing, a tool long used by academics to uncover biases that exist even beneath consciousness.

For updates and copy/paste prompt text visit rogerdooley.com/engine.

Chapter 5

Implicit Testing

There's no simpler way to get neuromarketing insights than implicit testing. The premise is simple. Precisely time how long it takes a subject to make various associations and compare those times. The more quickly the subject responds to an association, the more that association already exists in their conscious or subconscious mind.

For example, think about the stereotypical CEO. If you ask AI to create a picture of a CEO behind a desk, you'll likely get an image of a man. That's the more probable gender based on CEO mentions on the internet. Our brains work the same way. Since the vast majority of CEOs we've met or read about are male, even individuals with no gender bias might visualize a CEO to be male if prompted to imagine one.

This means, in today's environment, a random sample of subjects might take a few milliseconds longer to match "CEO" with "female" than with "male." This doesn't indicate they are biased but rather demonstrates some mix of experience and societal expectations.

This type of test is particularly useful for measuring topics like brand image. One would expect subjects to more quickly pair "innovative" with Apple or Tesla than, say, Kodak or Colgate. Ask people, "What do you think about my brand?" and you may get positive, people-pleasing replies. An implicit test, though, may show they associate your brand more readily with "old-fashioned" and "boring" than "creative" and "youth-oriented." If your target market is teens, you've got some work to do.

Limitations of Implicit Testing

Implicit testing is useful for a fairly narrow range of marketing questions since it measures preexisting associations. More importantly, those associations don't necessarily predict beliefs, much less behavior.[1]

Author Malcolm Gladwell is multiracial and an avowed liberal. He was surprised that an implicit association test showed he apparently harbored an unconscious preference for white people.[2] The results of the test may have been valid, but they did not indicate his conscious feelings about races. More importantly, they did not mean he was likely to engage in racist behavior, vote for political candidates who matched his unconscious preference, etc.

As Freud might say, sometimes an association is just an association.

How to Get Started with Implicit Testing

It has limitations, but implicit testing is one way to uncover how people feel about your brand. Or, for that matter, your competitors. If you want to see how the test works, you can try the Harvard Implicit Association Test.[3] It has tests related mostly to racial and ethnic bias but is a good example of the methodology.

Despite the simplicity of the concept, there are surprisingly few options for budget-friendly testing. Companies like Sentient Decision Science, Cloud Army, and iMotions offer implicit testing but only as a part of enterprise-oriented bundles.

Testable has (among other tools) an implicit test creator.[4] Similarly, Millisecond's Inquisit platform offers many implicit test variations, some customizable for your purposes.[5] But these general testing platforms won't provide guidance on how to use the tool for marketing. (Tip: your favorite AI model can help you fill in the templates with options that will help uncover the associations you are looking for.)

For marketers who are technically inclined, GitHub has a plethora of publicly available tests for various platforms.[6]

Unfortunately, at the moment the choice for marketers wanting to use implicit testing is between do-it-yourself options and more expensive platforms offering multiple methodologies. I'm hopeful that some entrepreneur will fill the gap with an affordable SaaS product that makes it easy for marketers to determine how customers see their brand.

When to Use Implicit Testing

Marketers use implicit testing when they want to uncover what people really feel but might not say out loud. Sometimes, as in the Gladwell example, people might not even be aware of these feelings themselves. Unlike surveys or focus groups, implicit tools reveal quick, automatic associations in the brain. They're especially useful for testing brand perceptions, ad effectiveness, or sensitive topics where people might give "polite" or socially acceptable answers.

What's Next

By now, we've covered the main categories of affordable, readily accessible tools for marketers wanting to dig deeper than surveys and focus groups allow. But we're not quite ready to leave the topic. In the next chapter, we'll look at a few emerging technologies that may provide even more insights in the coming years.

For updates and copy/paste prompt text visit rogerdooley.com/engine.

Chapter 6

Evolving Neuromarketing 2.0 Tools

Some neuromarketing tools haven't quite broken through the cost and accessibility barriers but may do so in the near future. In this chapter, I'll highlight a few worth watching.

EEG Testing

EEG brain wave measurements have been a staple of neuromarketing studies since the field's earliest days. (See the Appendix for more on EEG.) The problem has been to turn this technology into a cost-effective tool readily applied in remote settings.

The challenges are twofold. First, the best EEG studies are conducted with caps or helmets studded with dozens of wet electrodes. To be fit into our criteria for Neuromarketing 2.0, one would need something simpler like a Bluetooth headset with a small number of dry electrodes. Ideally, the headset should be able to be put on by the subjects themselves without careful placement.

The second challenge is that EEG setups produce a massive amount of data. Each electrode is a channel generating hundreds of data points per second. To be useful for non-expert users, an app or software needs to turn this firehose of data into just a few meaningful signals.

EEG Hardware Progress

Early attempts to use simple EEG devices like a headband with one or two electrodes failed. They simply didn't provide useful data for marketing studies.

Work is continuing, though. Companies like Emotiv make sophisticated EEG caps but have also introduced less complex devices: a simple 5-channel EEG headset, 2-channel EEG headphones, and 2-channel EEG earbuds. Currently, these devices are marketed for consumer applications like mental state monitoring and meditation.

Similarly, brands like Muse and NeuroSky make simple EEG headsets for consumers. These can interface with apps for meditation and stress relief, but there are no tools to use them for neuromarketing studies. Furthermore, even when these tools are used for their primary applications, customer reviews are mixed at best.

Can these or other simple EEG devices be turned into tools for neuromarketing? At first, it seems unlikely since the validated studies using EEG collect vastly more data from many more localized sensors. But perhaps eventually machine learning tools will find a way to interpret the smaller data flow from a small number of sensors into a signal useful for marketers.

Virtual and Augmented Reality

Virtual and augmented reality represent potentially game-changing technologies for neuromarketing, but they're not quite affordable or accessible enough to be part of Neuromarketing 2.0.

Today, some companies are combining VR with conventional neuromarketing tools to test everything from store layouts to emotional engagement. For example, Dutch neuromarketing firm Unravel Research combines VR environments with EEG brain monitoring from iMotions to test retail displays and point-of-sale materials, allowing brands to optimize store experiences without physically rearranging anything.[1] Meta has partnered with neuromarketing firm Neurons Inc. to study how people emotionally respond to virtual conversations compared to in-person ones, using EEG to measure cognitive load and emotional intensity during VR experiences.[2]

The promise for smaller businesses is intriguing. If VR headsets become as common as smartphones, we might see affordable research platforms that let you upload your package design or store layout and get instant feedback from consumers in virtual environments. Almost any immersive experience could be combined with, say, biometrics or eye tracking, to produce robust engagement data. The Meta Quest 3 already costs less than a smartwatch. The Apple Vision Pro costs more than ten times as much, but actually has built-in eye-tracking technology. So far, the software and testing infrastructure haven't caught up.

My prediction: in the coming years, we'll see "VR testing as a service" platforms that work like today's webcam eye-tracking tools. You'll upload your designs or content, recruit participants who already own headsets, and get back rich behavioral data about how people interact with your products, environments, or content in realistic virtual spaces.

What's Next: From Insight to Influence

You've now got new, affordable tools to understand your customers' true preferences and predict their behaviors. You can learn what catches (or doesn't catch) your customers' eyes from eye tracking. You can know what they find truly engaging from wearable biometrics. You can determine the emotions your content, product, or brand triggers from facial coding.

The kind of insights that were reserved for big brands until the last few years are now available to you. But that's just one part of

Neuromarketing 2.0. For decades, marketers have used behavioral science, consumer psychology, and science-based persuasion to improve their results.

These tools have been available to any size organization. Using them is essentially free. In most cases, they involve only different messaging or imagery we expect to improve results based on our understanding of how our human brains make decisions. You don't need extensive research to know that a testimonial from LeBron James will help you sell more of your basketball shoes—he's an authority in that space.

Big companies still have had an advantage, though. They could hire behavioral scientists to build nudge units to offer advice whenever and wherever they needed it. Their consumer psychologists could develop detailed customer personas for more targeted marketing. When they lacked internal expertise, they could bring in expensive consultants. In contrast, organizations lacking big budgets had to rely on already busy marketers reading books and trying to apply what they could remember.

In Part III, we'll see how AI is leveling the playing field. Today, even a solopreneur can draw on near-infinite expertise to optimize their marketing. Doing this can be accomplished in far less time and at negligible expense—exactly the way Neuromarketing 2.0 should work.

For updates and copy/paste prompt text visit rogerdooley.com/engine.

Part III

AI-Powered Persuasion

"Most people don't have the power of persuasion."
—James Altucher, entrepreneur, podcaster,
and author of *Choose Yourself*

Chapter 7

Your AI Behavioral Science Dream Team

Do you feel like there are some gaps in your knowledge of behavioral science? Would you be hard pressed to recite Cialdini's seven principles of influence, or name more than a handful of common cognitive biases? Can you explain the difference between the availability heuristic and the representativeness heuristic? No worries! In the next few minutes, I'll show you how to use AI to use powerful behavioral science principles to help you write a headline that outperforms your current one.

But first, let me tell you how I'm working myself out of my job with this book.

I avoid most consulting engagements. Why? Problems like scope creep, where client expectations metastasize as the project progresses. Interminable meetings, whether in-person or virtual. Deliverables that, once delivered, end up gathering dust on a bookshelf. Recommendations that would transform performance but are never implemented due to corporate indecision. When approached for an engagement, I'm happy to recommend colleagues who enjoy that sort of work.

Despite my best efforts, though, I've occasionally agreed to do a review of a marketing program or a website with a goal of recommending improvements based on behavioral science and persuasion psychology. (More often than not, I find the solutions to poor performance in these situations aren't related to psychological leverage. Instead, they are simpler things like fixing terrible user experience, unclear calls to action, and so on. But that's another story.)

I actually enjoy the work of finding creative ways to apply consumer psychology, behavior design, etc. to solve a problem or improve performance. It's the corporate friction that goes along with these projects that I don't like.

The bad news: hiring me or my colleagues at consulting firms specializing in behavioral persuasion isn't cheap. It may be an affordable expense for larger companies, but for smaller companies, nonprofits, startups, etc., the cost can be prohibitive. Even in large companies, individual business units, departments, product managers, etc., often face budget constraints.

The good news: now, you don't have to hire me.

Your New Million-Dollar Team (That Costs Less Than Lunch)

Right now, today, you have access to the collective knowledge of every behavioral scientist and persuasion expert who's ever published their work. Daniel Kahneman's decades of research on cognitive biases? It's in there. Robert Cialdini's principles of influence? Check. BJ Fogg's Behavior Model? Got it. The latest studies from other researchers on pricing psychology, social proof, and emotional triggers? Yep, them too.

This isn't hypothetical. Here's a quick experiment you can try.

Open ChatGPT, Claude, Gemini, or whichever AI tool you prefer. Copy and paste this prompt, either as is or by substituting your own data:

```
You are a conversion expert very familiar with the
seven principles of influence described by Robert
Cialdini, author of Influence and Pre-Suasion.
I'm selling [project management software] to
[small marketing agencies]. My current headline
is ["Powerful Project Management for Modern
Agencies."] Apply Cialdini's principles of
influence to write 5 better headlines. Explain
which principle each uses.
```

Did you try this with your own business info and headline? If you did, you probably got at least one or two ideas worth building on. Of course, you don't have to stop with the first result. You could:

- Tell the AI to try again, as many times as you like—you'll get different variations each time.
- Ask for variations on the one you liked best.
- Ask for more ideas using a specific principle, like social proof.
- Ask for subhead suggestions that use a different principle from your top choice.
- Ask for image suggestions that support your preferred headline.

This kind of interaction would cost thousands of dollars from a typical human consultant. The back-and-forth could take days. And humans don't iterate for free—at some point, even the most generous consultant is going to say "enough is enough" based on the original scope.

Your AI, on the other hand, produced its first result in seconds. Adding iterations and follow-up questions added at most a few minutes.

One other important fact: you got more than headline suggestions. You also got a quick lesson in applied psychology. When it gave you a headline idea that used social proof, the AI then explained how social proof works for your specific audience. Your AI is increasing your own persuasion IQ.

It's Not About the AI, It's About the Expert

"Which AI model will give me the best results?" is the wrong question. With today's most sophisticated LLMs, your results will depend far more on your prompting and expert role definition.

Why? AI doesn't think. It matches patterns. When you tell AI to "improve my headline," it matches against millions of headlines it's seen, good and bad. Maybe it will bring in some headline writing concepts it ingested. Regardless, generic prompting gets generic, mediocre results.

But when you tell AI to think like an expert in applying Robert Cialdini's ideas, it's pattern matching against everything related to Cialdini the AI trained on. His books, articles, and scientific papers. Podcasts and interviews he participated in. Other studies and innumerable articles that cited his work. You're getting Cialdini's expertise, tailored to your specific situation.

Generic Prompts Give Generic Results

Let me show you the difference between a generic prompt and one that names an expert:

A generic prompt might be, "Improve this headline: 'Save Time with Our Software.'" That might yield a generic result like, "Revolutionize Your Workflow with Cutting-Edge Software." Is that better? Maybe, maybe not. If you keep iterating five suggestions at a time, maybe you'll get a winner. When I lived in Tennessee, people would say, "Even a blind hog finds some acorns."

Here's a better, albeit very simple, prompt: "You are Daniel Kahneman, Nobel Prize winner and expert on cognitive biases. Improve this headline: 'Save Time with Our Software.'"

I tried this in ChatGPT, and got, "You're Losing 10+ Hours a Week—Here's How to Get Them Back." That was the first of several and was a nice use of loss aversion, one of Kahneman's most significant biases. Other headlines used System 1 thinking and different cognitive biases. Even this trivially simple prompt produced a reasonable result.

The second headline doesn't just sound better, it's more likely to get results because it appeals to a fundamental, well-documented aspect of human nature. And you didn't need to hire a behavioral science consultant to come up with it.

A Quick Caution on All-Knowing AI

The massive amount of data the big AI models consume is mostly a positive thing. I've read Cialdini's and Kahneman's books, and I certainly don't remember every detail. I don't even remember every detail of what *I've* written. Once in a while, someone will ask about a blog article I wrote a dozen years ago, and I'll draw a blank on the specifics. AI can do much better than a human in that respect.

But all that knowledge can be problematic at times. Here's a glitch I run into often, even today. Robert Cialdini wrote about six principles in his 1984 book, *Influence*. This was true for subsequent editions of the book. Research papers and articles talked about six principles.

In 2016, Cialdini's *Pre-Suasion* was released. It added a seventh principle, Unity. This was big news in the persuasion psychology world, roughly equivalent to Moses adding an eleventh Commandment. But it took a while for this to become broadly known. For years after that, articles and online discussions still commonly referred to just six principles.

Why does this matter? It means that vast majority of the data the AI models have trained on refers to the first six principles. Since generative AI works on probability, even advanced models won't always consider all seven principles. This kind of error seems to happen less often today, but it's something to watch for.

Ask a human expert in persuasion and there's a near 100% probability they will count seven principles, even if they spent many years knowing only the first six.

Here's another example . . . In 2012, prominent researchers published a study that showed having people sign a form at the beginning produced more honest answers than if they signed at the end.[1] The paper was widely cited, but after difficulties with replication and allegations of serious data problems, it was withdrawn. Subsequent research has been unable to demonstrate the effect.

I asked four LLMs, "Does having people sign a form at the beginning yield more honest answers than if they sign at the end?" Two, Claude and Gemini, said, "No," mentioning the withdrawal of the original paper. ChatGPT said, "Yes," but qualified the answer with a comment about mixed replication results. Grok answered, "Yes," citing the original work and offering explanations for the effect. This isn't a recommendation for or an indictment of specific models. It's entirely possible that I would have gotten different answers had I tried asking again, rephrased the question, or used a different variation of each LLM. Rather, it's a caution against blindly trusting what seem to be authoritative answers.

As I'll try to repeat often, AI isn't perfect. It can make mistakes or even make things up to fill in gaps in its knowledge. You, the human, are responsible for ensuring no errors creep into your work.

Building Your Dream Team

Don't stop with one expert. Bring in two, three, or more and get them to collaborate.

Let's build your expert panel. Below you'll find some valuable experts to select from as you proceed.

I'll point out that this list is highly subjective and, for brevity, omits many deserving experts. If I've omitted your favorite expert in a field, I'm sorry. Feel free to add them to your panel. If I've omitted *you*, I'm doubly sorry!

Here are a few possible first-round draft picks:

Behavioral Science and Persuasion

Robert Cialdini. A researcher who went underground to study real-world persuasion, Cialdini is world-renowned for his seminal book *Influence: How and Why People Agree to Things* and his Principles of

Influence. Often called the "Godfather of Influence," he gives us timeless science-backed tactics (like reciprocity and social proof) that form a cornerstone for ethical persuasion.

Daniel Kahneman. Nobel Prize-winning psychologist widely regarded as the father of behavioral economics. Kahneman's groundbreaking research on cognitive biases and decision-making (summarized in *Thinking, Fast and Slow*) showed that humans often behave irrationally but in ways we can understand.

Dan Ariely. A Duke University behavioral economist and author of *Predictably Irrational*, known for revealing the hidden, illogical quirks in how people make choices. Based on deceptively simple experiments, his work helps marketers understand non-conscious drivers behind purchasing decisions.

Richard Thaler. Nobel Prize-winning economist considered a founder of behavioral economics, famous for the concept of the "nudge." Thaler's work, popularized in the book *Nudge* he co-authored with Cass Sunstein, demonstrates how subtle tweaks in choice framing—default options, simpler processes, etc.—can change behavior without restricting their freedom of choice.

BJ Fogg. Stanford behavior scientist and creator of the Fogg Behavior Model. A pioneer in persuasive technology and behavior design, Fogg showed the balance between a person's motivation and the difficulty of doing something was critical to making that behavior happen. His work was fundamental to my book *Friction* and is the basis for many conversion optimization and digital persuasion efforts.

Jonah Berger. Wharton marketing professor and best-selling author (*Contagious, Invisible Influence*). Berger's expertise includes word-of-mouth and social influence. His work explains why some messages and products go viral. He offers marketers science-based techniques to make ideas more shareable and "sticky."

Nir Eyal. Behavioral design expert and author of *Hooked: How to Build Habit-Forming Products*. Eyal's Hook Model became Silicon

Valley's template for crafting engaging user experiences. Eyal shows how psychology, neuroscience, and technology interact to keep users and customers coming back.

A few more. Also consider **Cass Sunstein** (*Nudge* co-author, other titles include *Manipulation, Sludge* and *Noise*); **Nancy Harhut** (author of *Using Behavioral Science in Marketing*); **Richard Shotton** (author of *The Choice Factory* and *The Illusion of Choice*).

You could stop here. But, if you are working on projects that need more specialized help, here are some more categories and experts:

Customer Experience (CX) Experts

Shep Hyken. A customer service and experience expert who has been a fixture in the CX world for decades. A frequent keynote speaker and prolific author, Hyken's books include *The Cult of the Customer*, *The Convenience Revolution*, and many more.

Jeanne Bliss. A pioneer in customer experience, Bliss was one of the first Chief Customer Officers and co-founded the CX Professionals Association (CXPA). Her books include *"I Love You More Than My Dog"* and *Would You Do That to Your Mother?*

Fred Reichheld. Known as the "high priest of loyalty" and creator of the Net Promoter Score (NPS) metric still used by the majority of Fortune 1,000 firms. Reichheld is the author of *The Ultimate Question* and *Winning on Purpose*.

Jay Baer. Author of *Hug Your Haters* and co-author of *Talk Triggers*, Baer travels the world speaking to audiences about ways to leverage customer experience for business success.

Matthew Dixon. Widely recognized for his sales expertise, Matt Dixon is also the co-author of *The Effortless Experience*, a research-based book that shows the negative effect customer effort has on loyalty. This research underlies many of the ideas in my own book, *Friction*.

Copywriting & Communication Experts

Frank Luntz. Luntz is a political consultant who showed how changing words can change minds. His book *Words That Work* teaches that "it's not what you say, it's what people hear." For example, his wordsmithing turned "oil drilling" (bad) into "energy exploration" (good) and the "estate tax" (sounds like taxing rich people) into the "death tax" (sounds horribly unfair).

David Ogilvy. Often called the "Father of Modern Advertising," Ogilvy created a style of copywriting that treated the consumer with respect. He believed in copy that sells with storytelling and facts, not gimmicks.

Chip Heath & Dan Heath. Brothers and co-authors of multiple bestsellers about psychology-based strategies, they make the list here for *Made to Stick: Why Some Ideas Survive and Others Die*. It explains why some messages "stick" in our memory and some even go viral.

Ann Handley. A digital marketing pioneer, an expert in content/copywriting, and author of *Everybody Writes*. She explains how to create "ridiculously good content" to grab attention and build trust. Her advice applies to emails, blogs, social posts, and every other kind of content.

A few more. Also consider: **Eugene Schwartz** (appears on many "best copywriters of all time" lists, author of *Breakthrough Advertising*); **Joseph Sugarman** (legendary direct-response copywriter); **Joanna Wiebe** (founder of Copyhackers).

Pricing Psychology & Strategy Experts

William Poundstone. Author of multiple bestsellers on diverse science-based topics, Poundstone makes the list for his book *Priceless: The Myth of Fair Value*. In it, he suggests that pricing is often a "collective hallucination," and explains how consumers' perceptions of price can be swayed by context, anchors, and framing.

Hermann Simon. A leading expert on pricing strategy, he's known for his book, *Confessions of the Pricing Man: How Price Affects Everything*. His ideas help companies scientifically set prices that are profitable but are still seen as fair by customers.

Dan Ariely. Also listed above in Behavioral Science, Ariely's experiments on pricing quirks illustrate tactics like the power of "free," the effect of "original price" strike-through labels, price anchoring, decoy pricing, and more.

Leigh Caldwell. A mathematician and economist by training, Caldwell is a consultant focused on behavioral economics and pricing. His book *The Psychology of Price* is a compendium of brain-based pricing strategies.

Dr. Markus Husemann-Kopetzky. A pricing researcher and consultant, and author of the book, *Handbook on Psychology of Pricing* which offers more than 100 pricing-related "effects."

Also consider: Melina Palmer (author of *The Truth About Pricing*).

Sales Experts

If you have an in-person or one-to-one relationship with your customers, you might need a sales expert on your team. Here are a few relevant ones from different eras:

Dale Carnegie. Almost 90 years after *How to Win Friends and Influence People* first released, it's still a top 100 bestseller (across all books) at Amazon. Carnegie's book might be the single best book on selling ever written because it teaches timeless ways to win trust and build loyalty.

Zig Ziglar. A sales legend, Ziglar became a best-selling author and sought-after speaker. He helped change the image of salespeople from pushy peddlers to trusted advisors. He turned his core idea of helping customers get what they want into specific tactics for connecting with customers, closing the sale, etc.

Neil Rackham. A researcher and consultant, Rackham led a 12-year study that led to his 1988 *SPIN Selling* book. It's a classic that remains in wide use today.

Matt Dixon. (Also listed for Customer Experience.) He's a co-author of *The Challenger Sale*, a bestseller that led to major changes in how companies sell complex solutions.

Brian Tracy. A veteran sales coach and author of *The Psychology of Selling*, Tracy turns universal sales truths into simple, actionable advice.

Grant Cardone. Author of the massive bestsellers *The 10X Rule* and *Sell or Be Sold*, Cardone is a leading contemporary thinker on sales and entrepreneurship.

Prompting Your Team

When you are faced with a marketing problem, think about which human experts you'd call if you wanted the best possible advice. Don't limit yourself to one kind of expert. Even if you are focused on improving your copy with persuasion psychology cues, adding a wordsmith like Ann Handley or Frank Luntz might enhance the results.

Then add them to your team and ask away.

For example, say you have a sales email that you think is underperforming. Try a prompt like:

```
You are a team consisting of Robert Cialdini,
Daniel Kahneman, BJ Fogg, and Frank Luntz. Analyze
why this email gets only 12% open rates and 3%
click-through. Each expert should provide their
perspective, then collaborate on improvements.
[paste email subject line and text]
```

I tried this on a random webinar pitch I retrieved from my email trash bin. ChatGPT gave a brief opinion from each expert as to what the email lacked and what would improve it, followed by multiple headline options (all markedly better) and rewritten body text.

This is very basic prompting. In the next chapter, we'll see how to seriously up your prompting game.

Testing Your Team

Different expert combinations work better for different challenges. What delivers great ideas for email subject lines might fall flat when you're redesigning a pricing page. The key is systematic experimentation to find what works for each type of marketing problem you face.

I highly recommend testing these variations:

Single Expert vs. Multiple Experts

Sometimes one focused perspective is all you need. A single expert can provide deep, coherent analysis without the complexity of balancing multiple viewpoints. But for multifaceted challenges, a panel of 3–5 experts can uncover angles you'd miss with just one voice. Try both approaches and see which gives you more actionable insights.

Different Specific Experts for the Same Challenge

Even within the same field, experts bring different frameworks. Ask Cialdini about your landing page and you'll get influence principles. Ask Kahneman and you'll get insights about cognitive load and loss aversion. Ask BJ Fogg and you'll get behavior design-based suggestions. That's an over-simplification, of course, but illustrates what is either a problem or an opportunity: the same prompt with different experts will yield completely different optimization strategies.

One way to get beyond the most obvious ideas from a single expert is to keep probing—ask for additional ideas, suggest a new angle, or provide more information.

Detailed Role vs. Specific Experts

"You are a marketing expert" gives you competent but vanilla advice. "You are Seth Godin" will likely yield his distinctive perspective on permission marketing, purple cows, and tribe building. The tradeoff? Specific experts can be more insightful but those insights are usually narrower.

As an alternative to your expert panel, try a role with very specific details. For example:

```
You are a digital marketer experienced in
[creating high growth for SaaS websites] using
[behavioral science, persuasive copywriting,
and conversion optimization techniques].
```

Prompted that way, your AI can draw on a wide range of knowledge to provide its advice. Try both approaches and see which works best in your situation.

Different AI Models with the Same Expert Prompt

Give Claude and GPT-4 identical expert prompts and you'll get noticeably different responses. Some models barely acknowledge role assignments, while others fully embrace the persona. Test your critical prompts across models to find the best match.

Here's a fun way to approach this. Describe the project you are working on to your favorite AI model and ask it for recommendations on which AI and specific model to use. I've received reasoned and useful advice this way.

Making Roles Work: Best Practices

Here are a few best practices for role prompting:

Be Specific About Expertise: Vague roles produce vague results. "You are a behavioral scientist" might work better than no role at all, but add useful attributes. Paint a more complete picture:

```
You are a behavioral scientist specializing in
online consumer decision-making, with expertise
in choice architecture and cognitive biases
affecting e-commerce conversions...
```

The more details you provide about background, specialties, and approach, the more focused and relevant the response becomes.

Combine Roles with Clear Tasks: A role without a specific task is like hiring an expert and then letting them guess what you need. So, pair the role with explicit instructions:

```
You are Robert Cialdini. Analyze [this landing
page] and identify which influence principles
are currently being used and which ones could
be added to increase conversions. Structure
your response with current principles first,
then recommendations.
```

Use "You Are" Instead of "Act As": This subtle change can apparently make a difference, at least with today's models. "You are Seth Godin" creates identity and authenticity. "Act as Seth Godin" implies pretending. Even worse is "Imagine you are..." The AI channels your expert more consistently and genuinely when you assign identity rather than request performance. I say "apparently" because this is common wisdom for prompt engineers,[2] but I've been unable to find actual research that proves it works. It can't hurt, though, so why not use it?

Prompt for Questions: This is an important one. You'll almost always get better responses when you conclude your prompt with:

```
Ask any questions that will help you respond.
```

Depending on the context you have provided, the model may seek to clarify details of your industry, your typical customer, your primary objective, etc. The answers will sharpen the focus of the response you get. For simplicity and to avoid repetition, most of the prompts in this book don't add the "any questions" line, but it's usually smart to include it.

Stay Relevant: Match experts to tasks logically. A neuroscientist for pricing strategy makes less sense than a behavioral economist. Don't try gimmicks. "You are a clairvoyant, 200 IQ marketer that can read minds" might sound creative, but it will produce less useful advice than a straightforward expert role.

Avoid Stereotypes and Demographics: You don't need to specify gender, age, or ethnicity unless it's genuinely relevant to the task. AI models are already biased from their training data,[3] and these details can activate or amplify the existing biases. Focus on expertise and approach instead.

Watch for Hallucinations: AI might confidently attribute quotes or ideas to experts that they never said or thought. Use expert modes for thinking styles and frameworks, not as a source of biographical facts. When AI says "As Daniel Kahneman said..." double-check if you plan to quote it or base an important decision on it. The frameworks are usually accurate; the specific attributions, quotes, etc., sometimes aren't.

Consider Multi-Step Refinement: For critical projects, you can ask AI to first create a detailed expert profile, then use that profile for your actual question. For example:

```
Create a profile of a world-class conversion
optimization expert who combines behavioral
science with data analysis. Include their
background, methodology, and communication style.
```

Then, use that detailed persona for your marketing challenge. It takes more time but can produce more nuanced insights.

Another multi-step approach is to let AI choose your team. For example:

> You are an experienced digital marketer assembling a team of experts to improve [conversion on a landing page for online image editing software]. The goal is to [get more visitors to sign up for a plan or a free trial]. Choose your team from top experts in [behavioral science, digital marketing, B2B sales, pricing psychology, and persuasive copywriting]. Name the five who will offer the best insights as a team, and name two alternates. Explain your choices.

Of course, you don't have to pack every discipline into one team. You could, for example, start with a team of behavioral science and persuasion psychology experts. When you find an approach you think will work, ask a team of persuasive copywriters to fine tune your headline, text, and call to action. If there are multiple price plans, turn to a panel of pricing experts for advice.

Don't Lose Your Star Players: Keep notes on what works best for you in various situations. And add role prompts that you find effective to your prompt library. Over time, you'll develop go-to expert configurations for different types of marketing challenges.

Put Your Team to Work

You now have a virtual team of world-class experts that would be impossible to assemble in real life. You've learned that results depend less on which AI model you use and more on how you define your expert roles.

Next time your headline underperforms, don't guess, ask your team. When email open rates disappoint, your composite expert can help. In some ways, this is better than hiring human consultants.

You can change your team expertise as needed, and you can iterate as much as you want without budget constraints or back-and-forth delays.

What's Next

Now it's time to put your AI behavioral science team to work on the marketing elements that matter most. In the following chapters, we'll target specific, high-impact areas where behavioral science delivers immediate results.

We'll start with quick wins, like email subject lines that boost open rates, headlines that stop scrollers, and calls to action that convert. Then we'll tackle bigger challenges like pricing psychology, web design optimization, and content that spreads. Each application will show you exactly how to prompt your AI team for solutions and provide examples you can adapt immediately.

The roles you've created are about to become exponentially more powerful.

For updates and copy/paste prompt text visit rogerdooley.com/engine.

Chapter 8

Advanced Prompting

Ask a barista for a coffee. Say nothing else. What will you get? Almost certainly, they'll hand you the simplest, most generic option: a cup of brewed regular, no cream, no sugar. If you were hoping for a caramel macchiato, you'll be disappointed. As obvious as this seems, that's how a lot of people prompt AI models.

The biggest complaints about the answers people get from AI models are that those responses are bland and generic. They are trivially obvious. They sound like AI. They missed the point. They are plain wrong.

Now, tell the barista, "I'd like a tall hot flat white with almond milk, an extra shot, two pumps of caramel, and extra foam. Oh, and make it extra hot, please." After an eyeroll from the barista, you'll get exactly what you expected. You specified precisely what you wanted and left nothing to chance.

AI prompts are the same. The more specific you are, the better your results. We're not going to do a deep dive into prompt engineering here but rather provide some general guidelines that will help as you begin to use AI in the chapters that follow.

You've got your expert, whether it's a team of persuasion luminaries or just one unnamed but highly specified digital conversion guru. You've got your model, or a few to choose from for the task at hand. Now, it's time to get your AI working for you by telling it what you need.

Frameworks Add Structure

Following an established structure for prompting LLMs is more about the human side of prompting. A framework forces you to think about both the instructions and information you provide the model. Following its rules makes it less likely you'll take a shortcut and get poor results.

There's no single framework that is universally accepted. The following sections describe a few. (Don't worry about trying to remember these. They won't be on the test!)

RACE (Role, Action, Context, Execute/Expectation)

Clearly defines the AI's persona, the task at hand, the surrounding situation, and the desired outcome.

Best for: Contextual, role-specific prompts to generate tailored, realistic responses.

AIDA (Attention, Interest, Desire, Action)

Structures prompts to attract attention, build interest, evoke desire, and prompt action. This is borrowed from the world of advertising and marketing. It's less of a general framework than a way of prompting for persuasive content.

Best for: Persuasive and marketing-related content.

APE (Action, Purpose, Expectation)

Clarifies exactly what the AI should do, why it matters, and what is expected as output. A simple, straightforward approach.

Best for: Purpose-driven explanations and focused analytical tasks.

TAG (Task, Action, Goal)

Clearly states the task, specific actions to take, and the goal or success metric.

Best for: Straightforward, result-oriented tasks.

Others include TCREI (Task, Context, References, Evaluate, Iterate), TRACE (Task, Request, Action, Context, Example), and CARE (Context, Action, Result, Example). I could list a dozen more, but I'm sure you get the idea. Following any framework will add structure and completeness to your prompt. We'll be mostly using variations on the RACE framework in subsequent chapters, but if you've had good luck with another, that's fine—use what works!

Six Rules of Thumb for Prompting AI Models

Before we dig into the details of how to craft a good prompt, let's look at a few concepts that are almost universally applicable:

Rule #1: Be Ridiculously Specific

The most common metaphor for an AI model is a super-smart junior employee who is tireless, but also forgetful and prone to occasional mistakes. So, provide detailed, step-by-step instructions for everything. Ask what you need to clarify as part of your prompt.

In human conversation, we take shortcuts when we know the person we're talking to has much of the same knowledge we do. People on the marketing team don't have to describe the company's customers to each other, or the features and benefits of a particular product. But your AI doesn't know anything about your customers, your products, or other aspects of your situation until you tell it. If you leave important information out when prompting AI, it will fill in the gaps unpredictably. Err on the side of being too precise.

Rule #2: Give AI Everything at the Start

AI usually remembers nothing between conversations, so feed it with all your context, data, and examples right away. Doling it out piecemeal in a long conversation uses more resources and is more likely to cause errors. Save chunks of information like customer profiles, marketing goals, style guidelines, etc., to make comprehensive prompting easier and faster. Using projects (Claude and ChatGPT), Gems (Gemini), or custom GPTs (ChatGPT) lets you save this kind of information for your AI to work with each time you prompt it.

Rule #3: Trust but Verify

The better AI gets, the more plausible its occasional fabrications become. Some elements of a reply may be completely fabricated. Other errors are more subtle, like misinterpreting Robert Cialdini's unity principle based on popular usage for the word instead of his precise meaning. We'll talk about ways to avoid errors, but *always* check any facts or recommendations that you plan to rely on. Ask for citations and links and then check those—even realistic-looking, linked references can be wrong.

Rule #4: Save Your Best Prompts

Did you get great results from a well-crafted prompt? Don't lose it! Build your own library of prompts that work. I also save prompts from other trusted sources that I may need in the future. Continuously update your saved prompts when you find ways to make them better. And save variations of these prompts specific to different models when you see it makes a difference. For example, to get similar-looking images from ChatGPT and Ideogram, I've had to create very different style prompts.

Reusing prompts that produce the results you want is a huge time-saver. You don't want to reinvent the wheel when you need a similar prompt months later.

Rule #5: Introduce the Unexpected

AI is a pattern-matching probability engine, so results tend to be average and predictable. Saying "be creative" won't help much. My friend and AI expert Chris Penn suggests, "add a banana." By that he means you should tell the AI to include something apparently unrelated to the topic in your prompt. This forces the AI to think beyond the most predictable response and can get you better, more creative results.[1]

Rule #6: Kaizen Your AI

Your first prompt probably won't be perfect. Think of prompting as a conversation where you keep refining your questions based on the AI's answers. It's all about trying, learning, and improving. Moving between models may mean starting over.

When you have a prompt scheme that's working, don't stop there. Keep tweaking and testing to see if you can get even better results. When you do find better ways of doing things, save them. I use Claude projects for various tasks. When I revise something that it produced, I ask it to compare my revised version with its original and analyze the differences. When it does, I tell it to incorporate what it has found in the project knowledge. The continuous improvement process is not unlike the kaizen approach to manufacturing efficiency and quality.

Meta-Prompting: Let AI Build Better Prompts

Even if you are good at prompting, your AI model can do a more thorough job. Instead of writing prompts yourself, let AI write them for you. Here's an example of a prompt I recently used at the beginning of a project to analyze and improve an e-commerce site:

> You are an expert prompt engineer. Write a prompt, starting with "you are..." to specify a role to analyze an ecommerce web page for user experience and suggest ways to optimize it for conversion. In particular, consider the ideas of behavioral scientists including but not limited to Robert Cialdini (social proof, authority, etc.), Daniel Kahneman, BJ Fogg as well as conversion optimization experts like Peep Laja, Brian Massey, etc.
>
> The goal of the prompt is having an AI model like you create a detailed list of observations about the current state of the page and a set of recommendations that would improve the user experience and increase the conversion rate. Ask me any questions that will help you understand the task.

That's a detailed prompt to begin with, more than 100 words long. But when I gave this instruction to Claude, it came back with several questions to better define the task. With those answered, it created a highly detailed 400-word prompt. The new, much longer prompt added some experts I hadn't mentioned, and, among other improvements, defined tasks I hadn't specified, like creating an implementation schedule.

At that point, I could use the prompt as is, ask for revisions, or make edits on my own.

In general, the AI will create a prompt far more sophisticated than what you would have written. It will ask for information you forgot to include or that you didn't know was relevant. It will suggest experts you haven't thought of.

This is meta-prompting, and it's a bit like having an experienced prompt engineer with a behavioral science PhD write your prompt for you. You can, of course, run the prompt not just on the model that created it but on other models as well. Run the ChatGPT-written prompt on Gemini and see how the results compare.

In the interest of brevity and clarity, the prompts that appear throughout this text are fairly simple. If you are working on an important task, I recommend prompting AI to enhance it. Give it the original prompt, explain your goal, and ask for questions. You'll get a more powerful prompt. At the very least, append text like, "Ask any questions that will help you respond," to your prompt.

Share Your Knowledge: Add Context

If you hired a consultant to improve your website messaging, would you bring your home page up on the conference room screen and say, "What do we do?" as soon as they walked in the door? Of course not. You'd begin by explaining the business's current situation. You'd brief them on the industry, current trends, and level of competition. You'd explain your brand's positioning and describe your customers. You'd provide as much quantitative and qualitative data as you could before getting down to discussing the website.

Strangely, marketers seeking advice from AI models often skip this step. Perhaps it's because they assume AI knows everything already? Whatever the reason, it's a big mistake.

If you dove right into the website details with your human consultant, they'd probably say, "Wait a minute..." and start asking questions to better understand your situation. AI models, on the other hand, are programmed to be agreeable and helpful. Ask a question, and they'll do their best to answer with whatever information they have.

Without background, AI will give you textbook answers that are accurate enough but generic. "Use social proof." "Create urgency."

"Leverage loss aversion." This may be good advice but may also miss the mark because the AI don't fully understand your specific situation.

Start with Your Customers

The most important context you can provide is describing your customers as fully as possible. But don't just dump demographic data. Your AI model needs to understand your customers as three-dimensional humans with complex motivations.

Customer Profile Framework

You may or may not have all of this information, but collect what you have. Even partial information is better than none. Here's some of the context to give your AI:

- **Demographics & Psychographics:** Age, income, and location matter, but mindset matters more. Are they early adopters or cautious traditionalists? Risk-takers or security-seekers? If you don't have quantitative data, ask for input from the people in your organization who are in contact with your customers, like salespeople and customer service representatives.
- **Customer Goals:** What are they really asking your product or service to do? Remember the maxim, "People don't want a quarter-inch drill bit, they want a quarter-inch hole." The customers for your pool service don't want 7.5 pH water, they want a sparkling, inviting pool for their family and guests.
- **Decision Journey:** Who influences the decision? What triggers the search for your product or service? What factors stop them from buying? In B2B environments, the journey can be complex.
- **Emotional Drivers:** Every buying decision can have emotional overtones. How will this product make me look to other people? Will a bad choice be harmful to my finances or my career?

Is the product consistent with my self-image? Does it evoke nostalgia or other emotions? The multitude of possibilities clearly vary by the nature of the product or service.

Your Business and Your Brand

Your AI model needs to understand not just what you sell, but how you fit into your customers' mental landscape. Tell your AI as much as you can about your brand, both the way it currently exists and, if you would like it to change, what that would look like.

- **Positioning:** Where do you sit in your customer's mind relative to alternatives? Is your brand the leader? Are you seen to have the newest technology? Are you highly trusted? Are you an economical alternative to more costly choices?
- **Voice & Personality:** Do customers think you are stodgy but safe? Are you a cheeky upstart? Do you lean toward playful humor or formal clarity in your messaging?
- **Business Model:** What is your business model? Subscription vs. one-time purchase? Do you use long-term agreements or can customers change easily.
- **Unique Constraints:** Every business has unique features like specific regulatory issues, compliance requirements, cultural sensitivities, technical limitations, seasonality, etc.

The Industry and Competition

Just like a human consultant, your AI model should understand your entire industry ecosystem, not just your company.

- **Market Dynamics:** Is your industry growing or consolidating? Are customers becoming more or less price-sensitive?

- **Competitor Positioning:** How does the competition position themselves? What are competitors known for? Who's the leader? Who do you see as vulnerable?
- **Industry Language:** What jargon is used? Are there any terms to avoid? Are there evolving buzzwords that you need to mention?
- **Emerging Trends:** What changes in customer behavior or technology are reshaping purchase decisions?

White papers, industry reports, and analyst research are excellent training data for your AI. Competitor websites and marketing materials can also provide valuable context about what your customers are seeing elsewhere.

Let AI Unlock Your Knowledge

In a perfect world, you'd have detailed customer, industry, and competitor information at your digital fingertips, neatly formatted in documents or spreadsheets ready to upload to your AI model. Large companies often have that kind of data handy, but smaller ones may not.

Here's one simple workaround to get the customer knowledge you lack. Many marketers already know more about their customers than they realize. If you've talked to customers, read reviews, answered support tickets, or spoken with sales reps, you likely have insights waiting to be surfaced.

The Interview Approach

Use the prompt below to have your AI interview you (or a team member) like a curious, well-trained researcher. You don't need to try to create a customer profile from scratch. That seems like a huge and challenging task. Instead, just answer the questions, one at a time, and let the AI build a picture from your responses.

You are a skilled market research interviewer trained in customer psychology, behavioral insights, and product positioning. I want you to ask me a series of smart, specific questions to help uncover useful information about our customers—even if we don't have formal data.

Please guide me through a structured conversation to extract:

What I know (even informally) about our customers
How they think, feel, and act
What might influence their buying decisions
What emotional or psychological drivers may be involved

Here's what we're selling:

Product or service: [insert here]
Target customer type, geographic location, or market segment: [insert here]

Ask one question at a time and wait for my response before continuing. Assume I may not have perfect answers, help me clarify my thinking. Ask follow-up questions if needed to dig deeper. Your goal is to create a clear picture of the customer based on my answers. After we complete the interview, summarize my responses into a clear, structured customer insight report. Organize the output into labeled sections I can use for later analysis or prompting, such as:

Customer Overview—a high-level summary of the primary customer type(s)
Demographics & Mindset—any relevant characteristics and how they think
Customer Goals—what they want to achieve (both practical and emotional)

```
   Decision  Journey—how  they  decide,  who's
      involved, and what stops them
   Emotional Drivers—what they feel, fear, or hope
      when considering the product

   Use plain, practical language and avoid vague
   generalizations. Include any useful distinctions
   between different customer types if they emerged
   during the interview.
```

You may be surprised that you and your team have better understanding of your customers than you thought. You can have multiple people from your team, even those with different roles, go through the interview process. Consolidate these into one document. Or, have AI synthesize them into one profile.

However you create your customer profile(s), be sure to save the final document—you will use it again and again.

Missing Context? AI Can Help

Real-world marketing rarely comes with complete information. You might know your customers' demographics but not be sure about their emotional drivers. You might understand your product deeply but lack clarity on competitive positioning. Or maybe you're entering a new market where you have little direct knowledge.

Sometimes, simple web searches can help you find reports, articles, industry analyses, and other useful documents to build your context. But it will often be faster to let AI help collect and synthesize the information you need. As usual, strategic prompting is the key to success.

The Gap-Filling Framework

Start your prompt by establishing what you do know, then ask the AI to infer the missing pieces. Here's an approach that works across different context types:

```
I'm marketing [product/service] to [what you
know about customers]. I have data on [list
what you have] but I'm missing [specific gaps].
Based on typical patterns in [industry/
category], what would you expect regarding
[specific missing element]?
```

For instance, you might have plenty of demographic information about your customers and know their biggest pain points but not understand what psychological barriers to adopting your product might exist. Tell your model what you do have, and what gaps you want to fill in.

The Iteration Approach

Instead of trying to fill all gaps in one massive prompt like the preceding example, try iterating. Start broad, then drill down: First ask for general category insights, then request specific applications to your situation. This helps you spot when the AI's suggestions don't match your own knowledge.

Deep Research for Deep Insights

When you identify gaps in your knowledge, "deep research" tools offered by the major AI models can fill them in. Obviously, an AI model can't know the characteristics and behaviors of your specific customers from public information it can find. But it may be able to infer some of that information that will allow better targeting of your behavioral nudges.

For this task, deep research models will work best—they can do extensive web searching on each aspect of the task to create custom insights the regular models won't come up with.

Create Your Customer Profiles

Here's a prompt that uses basic data about your situation to develop the customer data you lack:

> You are a market research assistant trained in consumer behavior, psychology, and decision-making. I need substitute customer data for a product or service, because we don't have internal customer data available.
>
> Based on the limited information below, please generate one or more detailed, realistic customer profiles using publicly available insight, logical reasoning, and patterns of human behavior. These profiles will be used to guide marketing messaging and behavioral science interventions.
>
> Known Information:
>
> Product or service: *[Insert your product or service here]*
>   Target customer type: *[e.g., homeowners, office managers, parents, small business owners, manufacturing companies, etc.]*
>   Geographic focus: *[e.g., Houston, Texas; Midwest US; UK, etc.]*
>   Price tier: *[e.g., value, mid-market, premium]*
>   Delivery or purchase context: *[e.g., in-person service, subscription box, e-commerce, seasonal, etc.]*
>   Any known competitors or alternatives: *[optional—e.g., TaskRabbit, local vendors, brand X, etc.]*

Please Provide:

A realistic, research-based customer profile, or more than one if distinct types are likely. For each, briefly describe their demographics and mindset, what goals they want to achieve with the product, how they make decisions (including influencers and barriers), and the emotional factors that might affect their behavior. Present your findings clearly and concisely in plain language, organized in labeled sections.

Use sound reasoning and observation to infer useful details. This document should be grounded in behavioral realism, not fiction. Avoid vague generalizations and provide specifics marketers can act on, even if they are inferred.

Assume no internal data is available. Present the findings in clear, labeled sections, suitable for further analysis or prompt chaining.

This prompt, fed even with basic information, will produce a reasonable substitute for missing data.

I ran it on Gemini 2.5 Pro in deep research mode, and the resulting report was shockingly good. The hypothetical business was a pool service company operating in my small Texas city. It did a deep dive into local demographics, identifying two different communities with distinct age, income, and education characteristics. It read reviews that identified major pain points for customers. It looked at do-it-yourself options supported by local pool supply companies, comparing monthly cost and time required.

Ultimately, the AI identified two target customer profiles and provided psychographic characteristics of each. The 18-page report would be an ideal input to use in developing ads and other marketing strategies.

Researching Your Industry and Competitors

When you lack competitive or industry context, prompt your AI to act as an industry analyst. If you've got little or nothing to work with, try this prompt using a research AI model:

```
You are an expert industry analyst with deep
knowledge across multiple sectors. I need you to
create a comprehensive industry context document
that I can use for future marketing and strategic
planning. Please analyze the following:

Industry: [Specify industry, e.g., "residential
    solar    installation"    or    "enterprise
    cybersecurity software"]
Customer Segment: [Describe target customers,
    e.g., "mid-market B2B companies with 100-500
    employees"  or  "affluent  homeowners  aged
    45-65"]
Product/Service Category: [Specify what you
    offer, e.g., "subscription-based monitoring
    tools" or "premium installation services"]

   Based on this information, provide a detailed
analysis covering:

1. Market Landscape
     Describe the current market size, growth
  trajectory, and maturity stage. Include pricing
  trends, price sensitivity patterns, and whether
  the market is consolidating or fragmenting.
  Note any important regulatory considerations.
2. Customer Psychology & Behavior
     Explain the primary pain points, buying
  triggers,  and  emotional  drivers  behind
  purchases. Include their risk tolerance, typical
```

objections, trusted information sources, and how long their buying journey usually takes.

3. Competitive Dynamics

Identify the top players and their positioning strategies. Describe the market leader's strengths and vulnerabilities, common differentiation approaches, and any emerging disruptors. Include typical price ranges and value propositions.

4. Industry Language & Culture

List essential terminology, credibility-building phrases, and current buzzwords. Note terms to avoid and important cultural norms or communication styles specific to this industry.

5. Trends & Disruptions

Describe technology shifts, generational changes, economic factors, and new business models affecting buying behavior. Include any lasting post-pandemic changes or ESG considerations.

6. Sales & Marketing Dynamics

Provide typical customer acquisition costs, most effective channels, average sales cycles, and decision-making unit composition. Note seasonality patterns and retention benchmarks.

7. Success Factors & Barriers

Explain critical success factors, common failure points for new entrants, required capabilities, and the importance of partnerships or ecosystems.

Format this as a reference document I can paste into future prompts. Distinguish between established patterns and emerging trends. Note when information is speculative or varies significantly within the segment. Focus on actionable insights with specific examples where relevant.

Your output will be a multipage document with the requested information. The model you use and how you frame the prompt can make a big difference with this kind of task. Running that prompt for water well drilling in central Texas on ChatGPT 5 instantly produced a 7-page document. The speed of the response suggested that it was based on the model's existing knowledge.

The information seemed quite reasonable. But, when I asked if a deep research approach would be better, the same model immediately began a much more detailed analysis using web research. The report it created was about the same length but had reference links for every point—dozens in all. And the model offered to expand on various topics, including creating county-by-county cheat sheets (for fees, regulations, etc.), building a competitor matrix, and designing a lead generation strategy using SEO and advertising.

Clearly, additional knowledge like a detailed competitor comparison could be a great addition to your industry context. Prompt as needed to fill in any blanks. Or ask your AI what other information would be helpful for creating the best possible industry context.

However you prompt the AI, compare the information it generates to what you know. If you find gaps or errors, edit the document yourself or ask your AI to dig deeper on those particular points. Save the final industry context document for use whenever you are prompting for marketing advice.

Reality Check

The documents you'll get from these prompts are similar to reports that would cost thousands of dollars if you hired a consultant to create them.

But remember that AI models generate plausible-sounding ideas that may appear to be verified facts. Their "knowledge" comes from training data that may be outdated, biased toward well-documented (often larger) companies, or simply wrong for your specific situation.

Treat AI-generated context as hypotheses to test, not absolute truth. If the AI says your B2B customers typically have six-month sales cycles, but your deals often close in six weeks, trust your data. If your data differs from industry norms, those deviations might signal a competitive advantage.

If you use AI to fill in context gaps, validate its suggestions with simple tests. Do they match what your sales team hears? What your customer service people know? What you see in actual buyer behavior? If not, refine your context document with the real-world corrections. This process builds a more accurate context model that makes all your subsequent marketing psychology prompts more effective.

Learning from History

Your past marketing successes and failures are a powerful source of behavioral insights specific to your audience. Don't make your AI work blind when you have this data. Knowing what has worked and what hasn't is usually the very best kind of data to work from.

Your data may be in various forms—narrative reports, spreadsheets, exports from analytics tools, etc. Whatever you can find, feed it to your AI. A few things to look for:

> **Winning Campaigns:** What specific messages, offers, or formats consistently outperform?
>
> **Notable Failures:** What seemed promising but flopped in the market?

Customer Language: Actual text from reviews, support tickets, and sales calls

Conversion Metrics: What converts best? What does poorly?

Social Media: What content gets traction or even goes viral?

A/B Test Data: Which email subject line got more opens? Which landing page CTA did better?

If you are lucky enough to have massive amounts of data on these topics, run it through your AI to analyze it and create a summary. Your behavioral science AI doesn't need thousands of reviews or a million call center transcripts, it needs to know what customers like and dislike, their pain points, etc.

The more hard data you can give your AI the better it will guide your future marketing decisions.

Reusing and Updating Your Knowledge

As you collect this information about your customers, industry, etc., save it in easy-to-reuse chunks. If you find you are using the same chunks of knowledge every time, you can combine them into a single "context document." Every time you go to your favorite AI for marketing advice, you'll have all the background ready to go.

There's no single way to save these documents. Multiple AI models can access Google Docs, but you can also store PDFs in Dropbox, Evernote or any other tool you find convenient. Various text document and spreadsheet formats also work. Just be sure they are easy to find—you'll be using them often!

Projects and Custom GPTs

Generative AI models usually offer options for "persistent knowledge"—a way to keep reusing the same information over and over without uploading it or attaching it to each new prompt. Your customer profiles, company and brand profile, industry information, etc., are exactly the type of knowledge you'll want to use in this way. Every time you analyze a page on your website, you don't want to re-teach your AI model about your situation.

Currently, each model has its own approach, and each of those has pros and cons.

ChatGPT Custom GPTs. You can create a custom version of ChatGPT with its own name. Use it privately or share it with team members. Not only can you upload your knowledge, you can even define a role that it will use each time you prompt it. You could create a custom GPT for all your marketing tasks, or you could create specialized ones for, say, creating and improving sales emails.

For example, you can create a custom GPT, "Sales Email Coach." You can then upload all the knowledge you've created—customer profiles, brand personality, industry landscape, A/B test data, etc. You can also upload more specific content, like a "best practices for sales emails" white paper from HubSpot, or article content from experts in the field.

Finally, you can define its role as, say, an "expert in email marketing and B2B sales, well versed in behavioral science and influence principles..." Use as much detail as makes sense.

At that point, prompting is as simple as asking the AI to improve the subject line and text of an email you give it, perhaps specifying the email's objective or anything different about the recipients. The role and context are already there waiting.

Claude & ChatGPT Projects. You can accomplish something similar in Claude by creating a "project." You can name it and upload all of your customer profiles and other knowledge. You can upload topical resources directly related to the project's purpose, like a guide to optimum user experience on websites. You'll need to specify the role as part of your prompt, but the context is already there each time you return.

These projects are easy to tweak as you use them. If you find something in its responses that could be better, you can explain your preference and tell Claude to, "add that to the knowledge for this project." Always agreeable, Claude responds in the affirmative every time.

ChatGPT has a similar project feature available to paid subscribers.

Gemini Gems. Gemini Gems offer functionality similar to projects and custom GPTs. For users heavily invested in the Google ecosystem, pulling existing information into Gems may be simpler.

NotebookLM. Google's NotebookLM is a rather specialized tool for working with specific content. It's a RAG-locked model, which means it works only with the "sources" (documents, websites, audio, etc.) that you upload. It hasn't devoured all the information on the web. This can be a good thing—it's less likely to produce hallucinations or inject ideas from outside sources into its answers. But it's not going to have deep knowledge of behavioral science, email marketing, or other topics.

NotebookLM has been known mostly as a tool for turning content into easily consumed media like audio podcasts with eerily human-sounding hosts, narrated video slide shows, briefing documents and more. It wouldn't be my first choice, but you can experiment with uploading the same kind of content as the first two options and prompting it for advice. A more interesting use might be to turn, say, your uploaded information into digestible content like audio overviews useful for training new team members.

Update Frequently

Once you've built your chunks of important knowledge, you can sit back and relax... but not for long. Things like your brand positioning won't change much, but you'll likely get periodic updates like things on industry sales statistics or marketing campaign performance.

Be sure significant new data is added to the knowledge in a timely way, either as supplemental documents or by revising your knowledge chunks. The latter is better since you'll likely find new uses for the data and don't want to have to deal with "old" knowledge and multiple update documents.

Keeping your knowledge fresh will improve the quality of the recommendations.

Case Study: The Power of Iteration

One of the most effective things you can do to drive improved results is to create a feedback loop in your specialized AI tools. This works particularly well for marketing areas where you get fast feedback on what's working and what's not, like social media or email marketing.

Here's an example. I wanted to improve my engagement on LinkedIn content. Nothing is more frustrating than devoting time and effort to creating a thoughtful post and only have a handful of your connections see it. So, I created a Claude project, creatively named, "LinkedIn Posts."

I uploaded what I thought would be helpful to the project knowledge:

- A couple of months of my most recent posts, including interaction statistics.
- Several articles about creating engagement on LinkedIn from sources that looked credible—no spammy hacks for boosting interactions.
- Two recent quantitative analyses of LinkedIn content performance from sources I trusted.

I then had Claude create a "content guidelines" document for me based on the performance of my past content and on the other sources. I added that document to the project knowledge.

Overnight Success? Nope

I began using the project to review new posts and suggest improvements. Or to condense a longer article into an appropriate post length. Initially, I didn't notice much difference in metrics like views per post. They still mostly ran below 1,000, occasionally cracking that threshold by a few hundred.

After a few months, I did a few things that had a big impact in the long run.

First, I used a cartoon illustration for a post because I couldn't find a stock photo that worked as well.

Second, I uploaded all my posts and stats that were made after the first set of data. Once again, I had Claude analyze the latest results. Even though I hadn't reached any conclusions about what content worked better, Claude began to zero in on how my better-performing posts were different.

The posts that got comments and shares had a few things in common:

- They tended to include behavioral science insights—on brand for me.
- They often were based on timely news about a recognized brand—people had opinions.
- They often included a somewhat humorous illustration—this stood out in a sea of sameness.

These new insights helped me with topic selection and helped the Claude project provide better advice, summaries, etc.

I repeated the process by uploading newer post data. Again, Claude crunched the new information, and we updated the guidelines in the project knowledge.

In a short time, most of my posts that followed the guidelines were garnering thousands of views, sometimes tens of thousands. Some got hundreds of thousands of impressions. Serious LinkedIn influencers might not be impressed, but for me that was a huge jump—nearly 100×—from my baseline that had been mostly static for years.

The context I provided helped, but iterating with updated performance data was essential.

The Lesson: Iterate, Iterate, Iterate

The great thing about using AI as a consultant is that it doesn't keep sending you bills. If you had consulting firm come in, analyze your situation, and make recommendations, that would be it. If you got new data a month later, they wouldn't do a new analysis and revise their recommendations without sending a hefty bill.

That's exactly what I did with my Claude project, though. And updating both my results and adding new quantitative LinkedIn performance metrics is what enabled me to ramp up engagement so much in so little time.

Your AI tools aren't static. The models keep improving, of course, but you can add new internal or external data as soon as it is available. The advice you get will get better and better, without the incremental cost.

Making It Work in Practice

The beauty of this approach is that you build your context documents once and refine them over time. Each campaign, each email, each social media post teaches you something new about the psychology of your customers or audience. Keep adding those insights to your saved knowledge.

When you need quick advice on an email subject line, attach your context and ask. When you're planning a major campaign, attach your context and go deep. This will enable your AI to maintain consistency while it adapts its advice to each specific challenge.

The Multiplier Effect

Here's what happens when you properly give your AI the context it needs using your saved knowledge:

- Instead of "use social proof," you get specific advice on whether peer testimonials, usage statistics, or industry recognition will resonate most with your potential customers.
- Rather than "create urgency," you learn which type of scarcity actually motivates your buyers (time, availability, opportunity cost...).
- Beyond "leverage loss aversion," you discover the specific losses your customers fear most and how to address them in an authentic way.

The time you invest in creating comprehensive knowledge pays dividends every time you use AI for marketing guidance. With the right context, you're getting expert recommendations tailored to your unique situation.

Next, I'll show you exactly how to prompt different AI models to think like legendary behavioral scientists and apply their insights to your specific challenges.

Your First Mission

Let's put this into practice right now with a simple experiment. Pick your biggest marketing headache, or at least some aspect of your marketing that you know is underperforming:

- Emails with low open or click rates
- A landing page that converts poorly
- An ad that gets no results
- A product your customers don't understand

Now, run this exact process:

Step 1: Ask AI to identify which behavioral science expert would be best for your problem. We'll keep it simple here, but of course you could ask for multiple experts to put on a team.

```
Which behavioral science expert would be best
for improving [describe your specific problem]?
```

Step 2: Have AI create the perfect prompt:

```
Create a detailed prompt for [expert name] to
analyze and improve [your problem]. Include
what context and examples I should provide.
```

Step 3: Run the prompt AI created, adding your knowledge documents for context.

Step 4: Ask follow-up questions and/or ask for more variations.

This entire process should take less than 15 minutes. You'll be surprised that even this simple sequence can give you solid solutions to try.

This experiment is intentionally simple. If you are attacking a serious problem, use more advanced prompting strategies as described earlier.

Your AI Changes You (in a Good Way)

AI skeptics suggest that as we outsource parts of our thinking to AI models that our own cognitive abilities will decline. I suppose that might be true if you are letting AI do all your work and blindly pasting its output into your documents, emails, and so on.

I'd argue that using AI in the way I describe can *improve* your skills. You'll get better at exploiting the full power of AI, of course, but you'll also be picking up valuable knowledge along the way. You'll see how behavioral science theories are being turned into practical improvements to your own marketing. You'll get suggestions for A/B testing. You'll see first-hand what works best with your customers.

Your AI is getting smarter as you accumulate real-world performance data. And so are you!

A Quick Word About Ethics

The tools of behavioral science are effective in influencing behavior. We've known this for decades. Today, AI is a force multiplier—it can give you sharper insights and iterate more quickly. But these techniques can manipulate, deceive, and exploit. They can create dark patterns that trick people into decisions they'll regret.

Don't be that marketer.

Robert Cialdini's original research included going undercover to study the techniques of known persuaders like telemarketers and used car salespeople. But as he translated his findings into advice for marketers, he qualified it. I've seen Cialdini's speeches and interviews. I've read his books. I've never done a word frequency analysis, but I can tell you the word "ethical" appears very, very often.

Use these tools to help customers make decisions they'll feel good about. If your product genuinely helps people, behavioral science helps them realize it faster. If your product is garbage, no amount of psychology will save you. Using these techniques to sell it will destroy your reputation.

The best behavioral science makes good decisions easier. It doesn't trick people into bad ones.

Your Persuasion Control Center

Before we dive into specific applications, let's set up your workspace. Create a folder called "Persuasion Central" or any other catchy name you think fits. Create and include these documents:

> **Expert Roster:** This is your list of go-to experts for different challenges. This can evolve over time as you see which prompts give you the best advice. Add some specialists, like experts in

landing page optimization or persuasive copywriting. You can even include niche industry experts. (A car dealer, for example, might add Carl Sewell, an auto sales and dealer operations expert who literally wrote the book on customer service for auto retailers: *Customers for Life*.)[2]

Context Document(s): This is your customer, brand, industry, etc., knowledge we discussed earlier. Save as one big document or a few individual documents you can mix and match for different needs.

Other Resources: Sometimes, you'll find additional data that directly applies to what you are doing. This could be anything from a guide like Copyblogger's 56-page PDF, *How to Write Magnetic Headlines*[3] to a hot-off-the-press study of what goes viral on TikTok.

Prompt Library: Your prompts will get better and better. When you find one that works well, save it! Keep updating these as you improve them. One document should be enough to get started. Having your best prompts in one place is a huge time-saver, far better than searching through your saved history in multiple AI models. This isn't just for your marketing advice prompts. Save deep research prompts, image style prompts, etc., here too—anything you might want to reuse in the future. Label the prompts by model if you find individual variations that get the best results.

Results: Put your web analytics, social media stats, A/B test results in here. If the data is voluminous, use your AI to create summaries that you can attach to your prompts. As new data comes in, add it here.

Swipe File: As you visit sites, use apps, or read your email, you may run across things that other people are doing that you think you might want to try. Save them here and use them when you need inspiration. This is also a great place to put things that worked really well for you. Even if you'll never use that exact email pitch again, it might be the starting point for your next winner.

Once your "control center" is populated with effective prompts, customer profiles, real-world results, and all the other information we've discussed, it becomes your competitive edge. You'll be able to create more effective, more persuasive marketing in less time. In big companies there's a lot of fear about how AI will impact jobs. If you are seated at the controls, you'll have a lot less to worry about.

What's Next

You now have a behavioral science team that would cost Fortune 500 companies, well, a fortune. You know how to use them, how to combine their expertise, and how to customize their advice for your specific situation.

Next, we're going to take this power and aim it at the quick wins. These are the changes you can make today that will show immediate results. We'll apply proven science to your email subject lines, website headlines, and calls to action.

Ready to see what your new team can do? Let's put them to work.

For updates and copy/paste prompt text visit rogerdooley.com/engine.

Chapter 9

Quick Wins to Get Started

Most marketing fails for a simple reason: it's written for the wrong brain.

You craft logical arguments. You list features and benefits. You explain why your solution makes rational sense. Meanwhile, your customers are making decisions in milliseconds based on gut feelings and unconscious triggers they can't even articulate.

In this chapter we'll get you off to a running start in making your marketing far more appealing to your customers' non-conscious decision-making processes.

The Five-Minute Behavioral Audit

Before you change anything, you need to see what's broken. Here's the fastest way to identify psychological failure points in any piece of marketing:

Copy this prompt:

> You are a behavioral science and persuasion psychology audit specialist with the combined expertise of Daniel Kahneman, Robert Cialdini, BJ Fogg, and other experts and researchers in this space.
>
> I will provide you with a piece of marketing content—an email/website/ad/headline/etc.—and your job is to:

1. Diagnose up to three high-impact behavioral hurdles that are most likely dragging down performance. For each:
   - Name the missing or misused System 1 trigger, cognitive bias, influence principle, etc.
   - Explain briefly (1-2 sentences) why this is critical in this context.
2. Prioritize these issues in order of estimated lift—i.e., which change would move the needle most.
3. Recommend one concrete revision per issue: a specific wording tweak, layout change, or strategic adjustment.

Be concise, brutal where needed, and focus on what will move the performance dial. [Paste or link to your content]

I just ran this on a popular SaaS company's homepage using Claude Opus 4. Here is a summary the biggest problems it found:

1. Choice Overload Paralysis (Highest Impact)—Missing System 1 trigger: Cognitive ease and fluency
2. Anchoring on Per-User Cost Without Value Context (High Impact)—Misused principle: Price anchoring without benefit framing
3. Abstract Feature Lists vs. Concrete Outcomes (Medium-High Impact)—Missing trigger: Availability heuristic and mental simulation

In each case, it provided an explanation of what the problem specifics were. For example, the "choice overload" comment was triggered by the page featuring four products, each with four or five pricing tiers, and 20+ feature comparisons.

For each problem, it also suggested very specific changes that would improve the performance. The choice overload could be helped by a simpler pricing grid, for example.

This took less than a minute.

Go Deeper When It's Important

That level of analysis might be fine for an email headline. In contrast, analyzing and improving a home page design is no small task—there are lots of tasks the home page has to accomplish. Often, there are multiple stakeholders in an organization that all want to lay claim to their share of home page attention.

With Claude, I followed up the first prompt with a simple ask for three more:

> What are three more things that could be improved according to the criteria in the first prompt?

Always eager to please, Claude came back with three more areas that could be improved: missing or poorly placed social proof, a free trial offer that didn't offer an immediate benefit, and excessive cognitive load from describing 200 available templates. The detail in the explanations and recommended fixes was similar to the first batch.

The "audit" prompt can guide the AI to focus on what's wrong with the existing content and messaging. That may hinder it from thinking about things that aren't there at all but could be added to help. So, I tried one more:

> Still in your role as an expert in persuasion and behavioral science, think about the goal of this home page. Are there other principles, triggers, biases etc. that aren't being used but could be added to the home page to increase engagement and conversion?

The first time I ran that, I didn't specify a maximum number and Claude delivered eight. They included things like invoking reciprocity with an immediate benefit (e.g., a calculator for the time saved), using the endowed progress effect, exploiting the fresh start effect, and more. For each suggestion, implementation details were included.

Get a Second Opinion

I thought Claude's suggestions were valid, but wondered if it might be missing even better ideas. With a general prompt like the one we used, we're creating our own paradox of choice for the AI model. It can think about seven influence principles, dozens of cognitive biases, and innumerable "effects" uncovered by researchers.

Using the "fresh start effect" would never have occurred to me. It's a principle that says humans are more likely to adopt a new behavior at a temporal landmark like January 1, the first day of a new month, a birthday, etc. Somehow, Claude picked that out or all the possible interventions as something that might work. Impressive, but what might work better?

I decided to run the original prompt on a few other models. The results, unsurprisingly perhaps, were quite different.

ChatGPT o4-mini. This advanced reasoning model thought for a mere five seconds and came up with these ideas, paraphrased for simplicity:

1. Vague Value Proposition—Missing the System 1 trigger of fluency—a single, crystal-clear benefit statement.
2. Under-Leveraged Social Proof—customer logos are buried below the fold.
3. Generic Call to Action—Missing Loss-Aversion & Urgency Triggers.

The AI provided a detailed explanation and suggestion of the changes that would help.

Gemini 2.5 Flash. The lighter-weight model from Google came up with its ideas:

1. Paradox of Choice—overwhelming number of features, use cases, and product variants.
2. Loss Aversion is Missing—no messaging about the benefits that are lost by not acting.
3. Social Proof and Specificity—details, success stories, testimonials, etc., would be better than mere logos.

Gemini 2.5 Pro. The more powerful version of Gemini came up with quite different ideas than its sibling:

1. Cognitive Overload—too much information, too many choices, visually confusing.
2. Vague Value Proposition—lacks a clear conceptual model.
3. Choice Overload/Analysis Paralysis—separately from the first point, this point was about visual confusion.

What can we learn from this? While there was certainly some overlap, each AI came up with rather different issues as the most critical failures in the same website. Perhaps we shouldn't be surprised—merely hitting "Retry" on an AI model's first response will never yield the exact same response. Sometimes, it will be totally different.

I tried that exact experiment with Claude—hitting "Retry"—and two of the three key issues were different than the first reply. Interestingly, they did match issues suggested by the other models.

The variations in responses don't mean the answers are wrong. If we asked four human experts the perform the same task, they, too, would never come up with lists that match exactly.

Here's my key takeaway. Looking at the responses from all of the models, in my opinion *none* of them knocked it out of the park with their first three responses. Looking at the responses in aggregate—the results of prompting for more ideas, asking what's missing, checking different models—*did* produce a solid list of things to work on including a few quick wins.

When you are working with generative AI models, more ideas are always better. Ask for a headline, and it will likely be mediocre. Ask for ten new headlines, and something might spark an idea. By the time you've scanned thirty or forty variations, perhaps prompted in different ways, you'll almost certainly have a starting point for a killer headline.

Score a Quick Win with a Better Headline

Analyzing any element of your marketing using the prompting process I just described can be done in minutes, even if you iterate a few times or check a couple of different AI models.

Some of the ideas you'll see won't be practical. "Simplify the product lineup" may be good advice, but actually doing that might be an arduous process involving multiple decision-makers and costly externalities like revising marketing materials, training programs, etc.

Similarly, "Eliminate the qualifiers and disclaimers" might make customers more likely to act but require a complex internal negotiation with the compliance team or company lawyer.

Other suggestions may not, on examination, seem very likely to move the needle. Yes, human judgment is necessary.

But, you'll almost certainly find an idea or two that can be a quick win. Changing a headline doesn't require any new code and usually isn't controversial. So, for your first quick win turn your existing bland headline into a powerful trigger to act.

Headline Makeover: Loss Aversion in Action

More than one of the AI recommendations for my SaaS site experiment was to invoke loss aversion, a key cognitive bias described by Daniel Kahneman. Headlines often focus on what people will gain. That's logical, but it's also a mistake that can reduce conversion, email open rates, etc.

Humans fear losses twice as much as they value gains. Hence, framing a benefit as avoiding a loss will usually outperform framing it as a gain. Here's an example:

- Gain Frame: "Get 20% More Productivity with Our New Feature"
- Loss Frame: "You're Losing 2 Hours Every Day Without This Feature"

If your customers are typical humans, they'll respond to the second one at a higher rate.

Chances are, the AI that told you to put loss aversion in your headline will have suggested a specific new version as part of its initial analysis. Instead of running with that, it's worth iterating one more time. Try a prompt like,

```
You are still the role specified in the first
prompt and using the same knowledge of our
customers, brand, industry, etc. One of your
recommendations was to change the headline from
[insert original headline] into one that invokes
loss aversion. Suggest five new headlines, and
explain why each might work.
```

What if you agree that the headline is weak but the loss aversion headline suggestions don't resonate or seem off-brand, even after an iteration or two? Maybe they sound negative or scary (that *is* kind of the point!), or the boss hates them all.

If loss aversion doesn't seem to be right, try shaking things up a different way:

> You are now Robert Cialdini. Use the same knowledge of our customers, brand, industry, etc. as before. Change the headline, [insert original headline], into one that uses one or more principles of influence to spur customers to act. Suggest five new headlines, and explain why each might work.

There are endless ways you could change the prompts, but iterating at most a few times should create a new headline you can work with.

Stack Your Triggers

But here's one more way to further increase performance: stack multiple triggers. If you are going with loss aversion, add curiosity. Or authority. Or any cognitive bias. For example, in your prompt sequence, try something like:

> Continuing in the same role and with the same knowledge, rewrite the headline to use loss aversion and also create a curiosity gap. Suggest five new headlines.

You may get ideas like "The Dangerous Mistake 73% of CRM Software Buyers Make (It's Not What You Think)" OK, it sounds cheesy, but this headline combines three psychological triggers: loss aversion (dangerous mistake!), social proof (73% of similar buyers), and creates a curiosity gap. If the click-bait sound isn't too far off-brand, it will almost certainly outperform a vanilla benefit promise.

Your Next Quick Win: Level Up Your CTA

Another fix that can boost results is improving your call to action. Even today I still see buttons with default wording like "Submit," "Learn

More," or "Get Started." These are rational, System 2 instructions. They require thought. They don't nudge us to actually move forward.

Here's a prompt to try in your quest for better conversion rates:

```
You are a conversion optimization expert with
deep knowledge of conversion optimization
literature and research as well as the ideas of
behavior experts like Daniel Kahneman, Dan
Ariely, BJ Fogg, and many others. Recall your
knowledge of customer profiles, brand, industry,
etc. and the website we are analyzing. Then,
rewrite/redesign this call to action to
increase clicks: "[your current CTA]"
   Context: [what the button does]
   Provide 5 options ranked by psychological
effectiveness in increasing conversion.
```

I ran this prompt on the same SaaS site where there was a large, blue button with the bland CTA, "Get Started." In a rare example of different models arriving at the same conclusion, both Claude and Gemini had "Start Free—No Credit Card" as their top choice. Both recommended this CTA for reduced friction and fear of commitment and the Zero Price effect. The "no credit card" and "free plan" messages were on the website, but in much smaller type. These address key barriers to conversion, and the recommended CTA puts them front and center.

Other suggestions included CTAs like "Join 225,000+ Teams—Start Free" to leverage social proof, "Get My Free Account" to invoke the endowment effect. ("My" implies ownership.)

Here the quick win would be to swap out "Get Started" for "Start Free—No Credit Card." I'd be shocked if that didn't have an immediate positive effect. Of course, testing is always the safest and best approach. Even the most compelling interventions don't always work as expected. For a website with sufficient traffic for

A/B testing, several of the other suggestions looked like plausible candidates for further tests.

Try this on your own CTA on your website, mobile app, or sales emails. Five minutes of effort could give you a major boost.

Do Named Team Members Make a Difference?

When I ran the CTA experiments, I changed the role description to a "conversion optimization expert" who had deep knowledge of the work of scientists like Kahneman, Ariely, Fogg, and others. In looking at the results, I noticed using "Free," an effect linked to Ariely, featured in eight out of the ten suggestions. The endowment effect, also associated with Ariely, was part of one recommendation. Did my mentioning Dan Ariely by name prime the AI models to think about his ideas more than others?

I ran the identical prompt on ChatGPT, removing Ariely and substituting Robert Cialdini. The result? All five recommendations used "Free" in their wording, but there was no endowment effect idea or any other concepts closely associated with Ariely. One less obvious idea from ChatGPT was this headline, "Yes! Give Me 14 Days Free--No Credit Card." Beginning with "Yes!" was intended to invoke Cialdini's Commitment & Consistency principle—a concept neither of the other models thought of.

Based on this anecdote and other experience I've had, naming specific experts can influence results. But, if the prompt is reasonably broad, well-known ideas will surface regardless of who is named. Claude and Gemini weren't primed with "Cialdini" but both mentioned social proof. ChatGPT used "Free" in every idea, even without the "Ariely" prompt.

> So, include a few names of experts you think are relevant but include language like "and others" so you don't unintentionally limit the AI's thinking. To dig deeper and get less obvious ideas, do the opposite. Start with "You are..." and name just one expert at a time. A few iterations should yield multiple useful ideas.
>
> Throughout this book, some sample prompts name experts, many don't. Feel free to try adding, subtracting, or changing experts—each variation will give different results. Adding a lesser known expert or one from an entirely different field can force the AI to think harder and get more creative—that's usually a good thing!

Another Quick Win: Social Proof Power-Ups

Perhaps no other influence technique is more commonly used than social proof. Humans tend to do what others are doing, so things like customer counts or photos, testimonials, etc., almost always have a positive effect. But some work much better than others.

"Join thousands of satisfied customers!"—we've all seen variations on this. It might be better than nothing, but it's more an unproven, vague claim than effective social proof. Today's skeptical buyers aren't going to be persuaded.

Real social proof is specific and verifiable. It is from people like the ones you are trying to persuade. Social proof lives on a continuum with another Cialdini principle, authority. A testimonial from a designer is social proof. A testimonial from the head designer at Apple is authority.

Here's a prompt to find ways to make your social proof work to power your sales growth:

> You are a behavioral science and persuasion psychology expert with deep knowledge of Robert Cialdini's influence principles and the literature

> on effective ways to invoke social proof and
> authority to be more persuasive. Recall your
> knowledge of customer profiles, brand, industry,
> etc. and the website we are analyzing. Then,
> rewrite/redesign this social proof: "[your
> current social proof statement]" [Optional: "and
> all other uses of social proof on the website"].
> Consider options that include simply revising
> the text and options for different ways to present
> social proof. Provide up to 8 options ranked by
> psychological effectiveness. Before you begin,
> ask me any questions that will help your response.

Note that this prompt differs from a simple "fix this" command. There are multiple ways to present social proof, so in addition to a quick change to the text of the current social proof, we're asking for other options. We're encouraging the AI to look at the various ways we currently use social proof, like testimonials or customer logos. And we're telling it to ask us questions. It can't create new social proof ideas if it has no clue as to what you have available. (Well, actually it can... it will make stuff up. Don't force it to do that!)

The SaaS site I used as my guinea pig had very solid social proof already, leading with "Trusted by ..." and citing a large number of Fortune 500 companies. They had logos of prominent customers on display, a photo testimonial from a named customer citing productivity gains, and a montage of case studies from prominent customers. There's always room for improvement, but I decided to focus on a smaller SaaS company.

The new unwitting volunteer for my test had existing social proof in the form of a tiny "Trusted by 40,000+" line and five customer testimonials from small business customers. Both the business and individual who wrote the testimonial had names, and there was a thumbnail photo for each person. These are best practices for showcasing testimonials.

When I ran the above prompt on ChatGPT for the new site, it noticed both instances and applauded them, but pointed out two flaws. The "Trusted by" number signified plenty of adoption, but there were no specifics, logos, or brands shown, weakening its effectiveness. And it found the testimonials to be positive by showing real people and roles, but noted the language was very generic and lacking in concrete metrics or examples.

The prompt to ask questions would have been useful on a real project—ChatGPT asked clarifying questions about the audience, the desired action for the page, any social proof examples or metrics not on the page already, etc.

The AI recommended eight possible enhancements, including things like showcasing recognizable logos from customers, adding a "numbers bar" to highlight key metrics, embedding short video testimonials, adding a "Featured in" bar for press mentions, and more.

All the suggestions were valid. In the real world, I'd pick a few that I had data or content for and implement them first. Quick wins would be editing or adding text. Collecting video testimonials from happy customers would be an effective way to add social proof but would take time to solicit, record, and edit for the website.

I found it interesting that with each suggestion, ChatGPT provided sample HTML code to make it easy to implement. I didn't ask for that, but if this was an actual project it might have saved me a few minutes. This is yet another illustration that in their efforts to please their users (a fundamental trait built into the big LLMs), they will go above and beyond what you ask for. Sometimes the extras are useful. Run your prompts on more than one model and see how the results differ not only in their recommendations, but in the unsolicited extras they provide.

For your own quick win, use the prompt above, changing the details as needed, and ask your AI model to review your website, brochure, Facebook ad, etc., and suggest ways to make your social proof more effective. Or, more simply, give it your current social proof statement, like "3,500 happy customers," and ask for more persuasive variations. Making the right change to even a single line of text can boost your results in a big way.

Compound Your Quick Wins

Any one of the quick win prompts can improve your results. And each can take just a few minutes. So, don't stop with just one... stack your improvements to get results that go beyond additive and get into multiplicative territory.

When you add loss aversion to your headline AND make your social proof resonate AND rewrite your CTA to sound frictionless, you are on your way to turning a few quick wins into one BIG win.

Try It Out

Before you move to the next chapter, I encourage you to give this a try:

1. Pick the one thing in your marketing that most needs improvement.
2. Run a 5-minute behavioral audit on it.
3. Apply at least one quick win to it.
4. Launch it today.

Go ahead, take a break from reading and try it. I'll be right here when you get back!

What's Next

In Chapter 10, we're going deeper. We'll explore how to capture attention in a world where everyone has the focus of a hummingbird on espresso. You'll learn why your carefully crafted marketing is invisible to most customers. And how to fix that.

But first, go fix something. Right now. Your bottom line will thank you.

Remember: The best time to apply behavioral science was when you first created your marketing. The second best time is right now.

For updates and copy/paste prompt text visit rogerdooley.com/engine.

Chapter 10

Attention and Emotion

Is your marketing even being seen?

That's a valid question. Common internet wisdom is that each of us is exposed to thousands of marketing messages every day, perhaps as many as 10,000. I've not been able to find any hard data to support that number, but it's clear we are all constantly bombarded with ads and other messaging. Read a news article online you'll be interrupted by an ad every few paragraphs. Your Instagram feed is peppered with posts from advertisers. Even ignoring pure spam, your inbox is full of emails trying to sell you something.

We've adapted to this, of course. We blindly scroll past obvious ads. We delete emails without opening them. Humans adapt. But this adaptation becomes a problem when your messages are ignored before they penetrate the customer's consciousness.

This chapter solves that problem by teaching you how to work with, not against, the psychological mechanisms that govern human attention and emotional response.

Cognitive Overload

One big reason for ignored messaging is cognitive load—the amount of mental effort required to process information.

Your customers' brains are already overloaded. They're thinking about a million things. When they encounter your marketing, their cognitive capacity is limited, if not depleted. If your message requires effort to understand, it's easier for their brain to skip it.

To do a quick cognitive load check, try this simple prompt:

```
You are a cognitive psychologist specializing in information processing. Analyze this [webpage/email/ad copy] for cognitive load issues: [paste/attach your link or content]
    Identify elements that require the most mental effort or compete for attention. Provide specific recommendations for reducing cognitive load while maintaining persuasive power.
```

The AI will identify common cognitive load violations:

- Multiple messages competing for attention
- Abstract or complex concepts requiring mental translation
- Dense text that is difficult to scan
- Jargon that demands specialized knowledge
- Complex sentences that hamper comprehension

I ran this prompt on a SaaS home page, and ChatGPT quickly identified almost a dozen separate issues—competing CTAs, a big wall of random customer thumbnails that made the user scroll to see actual content, vague and confusing social proof, jargon like "context augmentation," and more.

The AI then offered a series of fixes that would reduce complexity and make the site easier to process mentally.

The Simplicity Paradox

When I last spoke to sales expert and *Effortless Experience* co-author Matt Dixon, we were discussing friction and why, even today, customer experience could be so complex and frustrating. He made a profound comment: "It turns out making things easy is hard."

The same applies to reducing cognitive load in your marketing. Making something simple can be surprisingly hard work. It requires understanding what you need to keep and what you can cut. You need to understand both your product and your customers' psychology.

But the payoff in results is worth it.

The more technical your product or service is, the easier it is to fall into the trap of using complex language and jargon. How often have you seen a technology provider lead with a word salad like, "Our innovative solution leverages cutting-edge technology to optimize operational efficiency across multiple business verticals" as their website headline or even part of their mission statement?

To the customer CEO who makes the ultimate decision, something like, "We cut your costs in half" is going to perform much better. It requires zero mental translation. The brain instantly grasps the value without having to work for it.

Here's a prompt to simplify your message without dumbing it down:

```
You are an expert in cognitive fluency and
processing ease. Rewrite this content to require
minimal mental effort. Aim for Grade 8 reading
level. Preserve important value propositions
and persuasive elements.
[your content]
```

I ran this on a statement of benefits from a digital analytics company. ChatGPT turned five jargon-laden bullet points into six punchy, easily scanned ones. Terms like "cross-departmental silos" became "separate systems." "Empower data-driven decisions" was simplified to "Make decisions based on data." Even a CEO could understand the new text.

At least in my little test, making the message simple wasn't hard at all.

Visual Complexity

Remember the eye-tracking tools we talked about in Part 2? They can highlight what your customers see and the order they in which they see it. And, of course, the stuff they pay no attention to at all.

Even without eye-tracking data, AI can help solve problems with visual complexity. The human eye follows predictable patterns, and designing for those helps customers see what you want them to.

The most common example is the "F-pattern." Much like the letter "F," when faced with an ad or web page filled with information, people in countries that read left-to-right tend to make a horizontal scan or two across the top and then scan vertically down the left side. When there's less text or content density, the Z-pattern comes into play: eyes move across the top, diagonally to the bottom left, then across the bottom.

Here's a prompt to see how your marketing content performs visually and how it might do better:

```
You are a visual perception expert who understands eye-tracking patterns and visual hierarchy, natural scanning patterns like F-pattern and Z-pattern, and factors like white space, focal points, directional cues, and size hierarchy. Analyze this, identify key problems that may hinder marketing effectiveness, and reorganize the layout for maximum attention: [your website, print ad, etc.]
```

Running this prompt with the smaller SaaS site through ChatGPT produced a host of recommendations for removing or shrinking distracting elements, making the primary CTA a focal point, and even a few text changes. This was in the form of a detailed outline for the top of the page ("above the fold") and the rest of the content ("below the fold). ChatGPT produced a wireframe for the new layout, and, when I asked, a simple image version of the recommended layout.

I would never hand the output of this prompt to a designer and tell them to run with it, any more than I'd take AI-generated text and paste it into a website. But the text description of the changes, the wireframe, and the image representation would all be useful in starting a discussion of what visual changes might increase conversions or messaging effectiveness.

Color Your World

Color isn't mere decoration. It can be a direct line to the emotional brain, triggering responses before conscious thought engages. Different colors can activate different psychological states. Here are some generally accepted color associations[1]:

- Red: Urgency, excitement, appetite
- Blue: Trust, security, calm
- Green: Growth, wealth, relaxation
- Orange: Energy, enthusiasm, affordability
- Black: Luxury, sophistication, power
- Yellow: Optimism, clarity, warmth

Two cautions: context matters more than universal associations, and these associations can vary greatly for different cultures. If you are working with a long-established brand, you may not have much flexibility in color choices. But if you are launching a brand or have a new product that needs distinctive branding, why not get some input on your color scheme? Try this prompt. If you have created your customer and brand context document(s), be sure to attach them.

```
You are an expert in color psychology and
emotional responses to color in marketing.
Recommend a color strategy for:

Product/service: [description]
Target emotion: [what you want them to feel]
Brand personality: [your brand attributes]
Market context: [target customers, geography,
    demographics, etc.]
Provide recommendations for:
Primary color for emotional impact;
Supporting colors for contrast;
Any concerns about cultural variations;
Best placement for these colors to maximize impact.
```

Color science in marketing has always seemed a little less robust to me than other factors. Pick any theoretically poor choice for a particular brand, like orange or red for a financial firm, and you'll find successful companies using it for their brand. But if you are stumped for a starting point for a new color scheme, the advice you get will be far better than nothing.

Open the Curiosity Gap

Want to know the one weird trick that will increase your clicks and email opens?

No guesses?

OK, I'll tell you... Start by saying, "Here's one weird trick..." Gotcha!

Viral headline writers have long known (and abused) the fact that our brains are curious. Very curious. When you create an information gap by suggesting to people they're missing something interesting or important, their brain compels them to fill it. Can you resist clicking, "Eleven things that will kill your chances for getting promoted... The last one will make you laugh out loud!"

You can definitely overuse this technique, and it may not be appropriate for all settings. But if your email open rates are lagging, give this prompt a try:

```
You are an expert in curiosity gap creation
and information theory. Create ten curiosity-
driven subject lines for this email. Remember
your knowledge of our customer profiles, brand,
industry, etc. Make the gap seem important but
bridgeable. Avoid subject lines that sound
like clickbait or will make the recipient feel
tricked or let down: [paste email text]
```

I ran this prompt on a pitch email I got that had a subject line starting with "Huge Opp" and was about children's books. That headline was indeed cryptic but seemed spammy and wasn't interesting enough to make me curious. I'd guess few other recipients bothered to open it, much less read and click.

In seconds, ChatGPT spat out ten headlines. Every one of them was better than the original, and not one was overtly spammy.

Instead, the headlines had just enough information to make the recipient curious enough to open. One was, "From Idea to Illustrated Book—Faster Than You Think." Another was, "The Hidden Shortcut to Entering a $4B Market." Plenty of candidates for split testing.

Use curiosity gaps for any situation where you need your audience to engage: email subject lines, article titles, headlines. Not such a weird trick after all!

Pattern Interruption to Get Attention

Daniel Kahneman showed our brains process as many stimuli as they can using System 1. Automatically, with little or no thought. If your headline or value proposition sounds like every other one your customers have seen, they won't engage. They'll scroll past, delete the email, etc., without a thought.

Pattern interruption wakes up their brain. It makes them pay attention by violating expectations. Try this prompt for a quick makeover of your headline or value proposition:

```
You are a pattern-interruption and attention-
capture specialist, combining the insights of
Seth Godin, Rory Sutherland, Drew Eric Whitman,
and other experts in capturing attention. Rewrite
this marketing message so it instantly stands out
from industry norms and is impossible to ignore.
Use your expertise to select the most effective
attention-capturing elements, whether linguistic,
visual, conceptual, or tonal, ensuring they grab
attention while reinforcing the core message.
   Message: [your message]
```

Providing all your context will help the AI's ideas. But merely plugging the boring headline "Maximize profitability with enriched customer insights" into ChatGPT with no additional information about the product or customers yielded, "Turn overlooked customer clues into profit explosions," and, "From spreadsheet sludge to pure profit fuel." Maybe not as clever as Seth or Rory would have come up with, but both will stop the reader with a combination of vivid imagery and unexpected wording.

Emotional Triggers That Drive Results

A lot of marketing tries to use emotion, but often it's the wrong emotion. It tries to make people happy about features or excited about benefits. But the emotions that drive action are more primal: fear, curiosity, belonging, and status.

Here's a framework for prompting your model to determine the best emotional trigger. As usual, be sure to provide your context knowledge—your product/service, customer profile(s), brand info, etc.:

```
You are an expert in emotional marketing and
affective neuroscience with deep knowledge of
the ideas of Mark Gobé, Jaak Panksepp and
Antonio Damasio. Analyze my customer's core
emotional drivers:

Product Service: [describe]
Customer situation: [describe in detail]
Current pain point: [what they say annoys them]
Desired outcome: [what they say they want]
First, think about the customer and what other
influences, hopes, fears, etc. exist beyond the
specific product/service. Identify their primary
and secondary emotional drivers. Suggest specific
messages and imagery that will trigger these
emotions.
```

I ran this prompt for a hypothetical provider of cloud-based project management software to Fortune 500 companies. I deliberately focused on the superficial pain point, projects that were late and over budget. The desired outcome was also surface-level: on-time completion within budget.

ChatGPT dug below the stated issues and identified the primary emotions driver as fear (of failure) and panic, part of the panic/grief system identified by Jaak Panksepp. The antidote for these would be giving the customer feelings of control and security, respectively. The AI suggested specific language that would help, like the headline, "From Project Chaos to Predictable Control." It also provided additional body text and imagery suggestions for each of its points.

Looking for emotional triggers speaks to what the customer really wants, even when they don't or can't verbalize it. The buyer looking for enterprise project management software wants reliable software that does what it is supposed to do. But what they *really* want is to not be embarrassed or even fired when the software doesn't perform or the project goes south.

Pro Move #1: Build on What You've Learned

The initial prompt will give you solid ideas about emotional triggers that will work with your customers. But, if you agree that the insights are valid, add this emotion data to your knowledge documents so that every time you run a new prompt to improve your marketing, the AI has this to work with.

Pro Move #2: Get More Powerful Insights with Deep Research

Digging into your customers' emotional triggers is one area where deep research tools can really help. They can source all kinds of information from customer reviews, competitor websites, marketing research and more to develop powerful insights that go beyond the obvious.

Run this prompt using your favorite deep research model for your deep dive:

> You are an expert market researcher familiar with emotional marketing and affective neuroscience. Your goal is to create a core emotional profile for this customer: [describe your target customer]. We offer a solution for this problem: [describe the problem/solution]
>
> Analyze market research, academic studies, and public online discussions (forums, Reddit, competitor reviews) to answer the following:

1. Emotional Landscape: What are this customer's primary fears and frustrations? What are their deepest hopes and aspirations related to this problem?
2. Core Driver: What is the single most powerful emotional shift they are trying to make?
3. Trigger Language: List 5-10 keywords and phrases that will resonate with them emotionally.

This simple prompt, run on Gemini 2.5 Pro Deep Research, produced a remarkably detailed 23-page report. I provided minimal information, merely specifying cloud-based project management software for enterprise customers. In a real scenario, of course, you'd use your context documents for better guidance.

The AI pulled information from dozens of websites and read dozens more without using them. The information came from all kinds of sources: consultant and market research reports, Reddit discussions, job recruiting sites, and more.

The report offered a deep psychological analysis of our project management software buyer, detailing their professional environment, core fears, and ultimate aspirations. It identified their fundamental emotional driver as the need to move from a state of chaos and vulnerability to one of control and certainty. It concluded with a detailed guide to the language and strategies that would resonate most strongly from an emotional standpoint.

I'd recommend reviewing this kind of report and making any edits necessary. It is AI-generated, and you know your customers better than an AI model. (At least we hope that's true!) But even as-is, a report like this would be a powerful addition to your context. Plug it into your project knowledge or custom GPT, and the marketing recommendations you get will incorporate the right emotional triggers and language.

Emotional Copy Persuades

When you write with genuine emotion, you evoke that emotional state in your readers. In a world filled with bland copy, words that spark emotion stand out.

```
You are a specialist in emotional contagion and
affective storytelling, combining the insights
of Elaine Hatfield, Lisa Feldman Barrett, and
other experts. Rewrite this copy so the target
emotion is not only understood but felt
viscerally by the reader. Use your expertise to
weave in the most effective emotional triggers—
through language, rhythm, and detail, while
keeping the emotion authentic and contagious.
After, explain the changes and why you made them.
    Target Emotion: [desired emotion]
    Current copy: [your current text]
```

Choose the emotion you want to invoke by running the prompt we saw earlier in this chapter. Better still, add the report generated by your emotion research as context for this prompt.

Chances are you won't need to use this very often. It's not going to help much with a paragraph of feature descriptions. But it can work well on longer form content and on stories in particular. A case study about a manager who saved two hours a week with your software might change from a focus on cost savings or getting more work done to something emotionally resonant, like being able to attend a child's soccer game or a teacher-parent conference.

I ran it on a case study for project management software. The story was reasonably engaging to begin with, but ChatGPT upped its emotional power by subtle reorganization, adding sensory words, highlighting personal stakes for the main character, and using contrast framing.

Keep Readers Moving Forward

Capturing attention is only half the battle, particularly if you are working with longer content. Keeping attention requires understanding cognitive momentum. Expert copywriters use tools like progressive disclosure (giving the reader bits of information), open loops (inserting questions to hook the reader's curiosity), and delivering value before the reader gets frustrated.

If you have long form copy on your website, in your email, etc., you may be losing your audience before they (or you) get to the payoff. Scroll-tracking tools can reveal how far your audience is getting. You might be shocked by how many potential customers bail out early.

Legendary ad copywriter Joe Sugarman suggested that your marketing copy should be like a slippery slide. Once the customer is on the slide, the copy is so compelling that they can't get off until they reach the bottom. Many of his ads featured columns of dense text, usually a recipe for disaster. But Sugarman's copy was so engaging that readers not only devoured all the text but were spurred to action.

To make your content keep readers moving forward, try this prompt:

```
You are a multidisciplinary expert in sustained
attention, cognitive engagement, and writing
persuasive copy. Rewrite this content so it
keeps readers hooked from first to last word,
using your best mix of proven techniques
including, but not limited to, open loops,
progressive value delivery, and cognitive
rewards.

   After the rewrite, list the changes you made
and the reason you made them.

   Content: [your long-form content]
```

This can be used for emails, articles and blog posts, marketing copy... any kind of content long enough that you are losing readers along the way.

The Attention-Emotion Feedback Loop

Attention and emotion aren't separate systems. They're interconnected loops. Emotion directs attention, and attention amplifies emotion. A good marketer leverages this feedback loop.

We've covered a lot of ground and plenty of tactics in this chapter. Don't try to use them all at once, any more than you'd try to use all seven Cialdini principles on your landing page.

Instead, experiment with a variety of prompts. See which ones result in ideas that resonate with you. Combine the most promising. And, if at all possible, keep testing new ideas instead of just running with them because you think they'll work.

Your Attention Audit

Before moving forward, go back to that underperforming marketing content or pick a new one. Run the cognitive load prompt and see what can be done to make it easier for your customer's brain to process. See if the curiosity gap prompt improves the headline. And take the time to run the emotion analysis process—these insights will help you not just in the moment but into the future.

Whichever prompts you try, find one change you think will work and implement it. Split test if you can, or at least watch the change from your baseline performance.

Small improvements in attention and emotional engagement create disproportionate results. A headline that gets 20% more attention can increase conversions far more if it better triggers the right emotion.

What's Next

Even if you get their attention and engage their emotions, your customers have to *believe* you to get real results. In the next chapter, we'll explore trust and social influence. You'll learn to leverage authority and social proof in ways that are authentic and ethical.

For updates and copy/paste prompt text visit rogerdooley.com/engine.

Chapter 11

Close the Credibility Gap

If you are a new company, or an established one seeking new customers, you may find your results aren't nearly as good as you expected. People open the email but don't click through to learn more, much less make a purchase. Potential customers look at the products on your website, maybe even add things to their cart, but fail to check out.

There are lots of possible reasons, of course. But, if you know your product or service is solid and your messaging has been optimized for your intended customers, the problem could be lack of trust. They don't know your brand well enough. Or, even if your brand is familiar, they worry that the product won't be as promised or that returns will be a hassle.

Amazon enjoys high trust through customer experience. They were a pioneer in letting customers post reviews so that shoppers could get unvarnished opinions on products. They fine-tuned their logistics so that their delivery promises were accurate and reliable. If I'm getting on an airplane Saturday and Amazon says the product will be on my doorstep on Friday, I order with confidence. And their returns are so hassle-free I'm comfortable buying even brands and products I don't know.

What about everyone else? Few brands are as well known as Amazon, and even fewer enjoy their level of customer trust. The good news is that there are ways to help customers trust you. And AI can help you find those triggers and optimize your marketing for maximum trust.

The Neuroscience of Trust

Before we engineer trust, we need to understand its mechanics. Trust isn't a feeling or a random emotion, it's a rapid calculation performed by ancient brain systems originally intended to keep us alive.

When someone encounters your marketing, their brain runs an unconscious assessment:

- Is this familiar or foreign?
- What are others like me doing?
- Is this risky?

This calculation happens in milliseconds, before conscious thought engages. By the time someone thinks "Can I trust this?" their brain has already decided.

Dr. Paul Zak is the researcher who discovered that oxytocin is the hormone of human trust. Higher oxytocin levels increase trust. Zak found that hugging someone, if it's not unwelcome, increases oxytocin levels in both people. (If you meet him in person, he's likely to give you a hug instead of shaking your hand!)

Amazingly, even marketing messages can increase oxytocin levels. And these higher oxytocin levels increase the probability of action.[1]

Digital Trust

Trust has been a problem since the earliest days of e-commerce. Before BJ Fogg became famous for his Fogg Behavior Model,[2] he headed the Persuasive Technology Lab at Stanford. In 2002, he published a paper listing 10 guidelines to boost website credibility.[3] These included things like making it easy to contact you, showing there's a real organization behind the site with cues like a physical address, a professional appearance, an easy user experience, highlighting expertise, easy verification of any claims, and more.

Savvy marketers today consider these as table stakes and take them for granted, but amazingly a surprising number still omit key elements and reduce visitor trust.

In the digital world, all customers have to work with is your website, your mobile app, and your reputation on other sites. Having all your digital properties optimized for maximum trust is a critical to success.

Getting Started: A Trust Audit

The first step in increasing trust signals is to see where you are at the moment. Your favorite AI model can help you. Try this prompt:

> You are an expert in building trust in marketing with deep knowledge of the work of Paul Zak, BJ Fogg, Stephen M. Covey, and other experts in building trust. Use your knowledge of our customers, brand, industry, etc. and perform a trust audit on the marketing materials below and analyze for trust signals. List any existing trust signals and rate their effectiveness. List any elements in the marketing that might act to reduce trust. Finally, provide a list of recommendations for increasing trust, including changes to the current content and possible additions of new elements. *[link or paste your website, brochure content, etc.]*

Running this on a local plumber website showed they were doing a surprisingly good job on major trust elements—a "Top Ranked Plumber" award from a national magazine, an on-time guarantee, a 100% satisfaction guarantee, a 4.8 star average review from customers, highlighting licensed plumbers with a license number, testimonials that named individual technicians, and more.

The problems identified were fairly minor, including use of stock photography, ambiguity about the local firm's relationship with the national brand, and a weak "About Us" page.

Recommendations for boosting trust signals included ideas like these:

- Add an "about us" video featuring the local owner and technicians.
- Add a "Meet the Techs" section with photos and short, friendly bios.
- Add customer stories, preferably in video form.
- Highlight local ties like involvement in community events or sports.
- Turn the "Why Choose Us" section into an easily scanned infographic with five key points.
- Demonstrate "competence" by adding educational content.

All of these seem like reasonable ideas. A few could be quick wins.

Use an Agent or Deep Research for a Thorough Trust Audit

Instead of plugging a website URL into a standard AI model, send an AI agent to capture more content. The prompt is similar but encourages deeper spidering of the website:

> You are an expert in building trust in marketing with deep knowledge of the work of Paul Zak, BJ Fogg, Stephen M. Covey, and other experts in building trust. Use your knowledge of our customers, brand, industry, etc. and perform a trust audit on the website below, checking both the home page, any "about" pages, and other key content pages and analyze for trust signals. Evaluate both visual design (images, color,

layout, accessibility) and copywriting (tone, specificity, transparency) for trust impact. List any existing trust signals and rate their effectiveness. List any elements in the marketing that might act to reduce trust or cause hesitation. Finally, provide a list of recommendations for increasing trust, including changes to the current content and possible additions of new elements. For recommendations, include an "Impact/Effort" table showing which actions deliver the greatest trust lift with the least work. Website: [your website URL]

Optional: Include a short competitor trust benchmark with examples of what others do better. Competitors: [Competitor 1 URL, Competitor 2 URL]

I used ChatGPT in agent mode to evaluate a local pool company. In some ways, the output was fairly similar to what you would expect from any major LLM. It spotted all the positive trust symbols like customer reviews, professional credentials, etc., and identified some elements that could be improved, like fewer stock photos and adding team member photos and bios.

The biggest difference was the thoroughness. In agent mode, the AI looked at the entirety of every major page on the website. It identified design flaws like a large and annoying contact form on every page.

Its best catch was a comparison table on a secondary page that highlighted the firm's high standards and practices in one column and used the second column for unnamed competitors. In the competitor column, all kinds of sketchy behaviors were listed, like urinating in the pool, peeking in customer windows, taking off their clothes, hiring illegal workers, and more. Perhaps this over-the-top approach resonates with some customers, but for most this bizarre, negative, and unsubstantiated content will reduce trust.

A more cursory review of the home page wouldn't have spotted this.

The Social Proof Spectrum

All social proof isn't the same. It exists on a spectrum from weak to irresistible. Vague statements like "thousands of satisfied customers" or anonymous testimonials are at the weak end. Much stronger are messages like, "71% of Fortune 500 companies use our platform." Or, even stronger, a video testimonial from one of those Fortune 500 CMOs.

If you ran a trust audit on your website, the results almost certainly commented on your existing social proof and offered ideas on how to improve its trust impact. You could run with that, or do a deeper dive as a follow-up question to the audit or as a new prompt:

> You are an expert in building trust by using social proof, social validation, herd mentality, and adherence to social norms. You are well versed in the ideas of Robert Cialdini, Dan Ariely, and other behavior experts. Use your knowledge of our customer profiles, brand, industry, etc. and consider changes to things like specificity, similarity, verifiability, and more to elevate this social proof from weak to powerful. Provide five variations, each with an explanation and ranked for expected effectiveness in increasing customer trust. Current social proof: [what you're using now]

Even a strong social proof statement like my "71% of Fortune 500 companies use our platform" example can be improved. Gemini suggested even simply adding a few big names could help. For example, "...companies like Apple, Microsoft, and Walmart use..." Even better would be adding an example with a quantified result, like "Hilton reduced customer hold time by 62%," or adding a case study from a relatable peer.

Sometimes you'll find a quick win, other times you'll spot a gap you need to fill, like a compelling case study to share.

Authority: The Expert Effect

Authority, another one of Cialdini's principles, is similar to social proof but more powerful because it's based on expertise. If I write a testimonial for your sneaker, that's social proof. If NBA star Steph Curry endorses it, that's authority. Like social proof, authority exists on a spectrum. A high school basketball coach praising your shoe is more credible than I am, but much less so than an NBA legend.

Other elements can affect authority's effectiveness. There has to be trust. We know that a professional athlete endorsing a shoe is almost certainly getting paid for doing so. Would they risk their reputation by promoting a shoddy product? We might trust LeBron James more than a random player we've barely heard of.

Authority can come from individual experts as well as organizations that provide ranking, certifications, degrees, and other credentials.

> You are an expert in building trust by using the influence principle of authority. You are well versed in the ideas of Robert Cialdini, BJ Fogg, and other behavior experts. Use your knowledge of our customer profiles, brand, industry, etc. and consider changes to our authority positioning from weak to powerful. Ensure the authority positioning is relevant to our customers' interests and is authentic, not boastful. Provide five variations, each with an explanation and ranked for expected effectiveness in increasing customer trust. Current authority cues: [your qualifications/experience, professional credentials and certifications, expert testimonials, etc.]

As with social proof, some authority cues may be quick wins, such as rewording a bland statement like, "20 years of helping entrepreneurs succeed," to "helped 100+ startups and growth companies, including two IPOs and three 8-figure acquisitions."

Microcommitments to Build Trust

Even if your marketing is loaded with trust signals, customers may not fully trust you. They will hesitate to place an order, fearing somehow things will go wrong. They may not fill out your contact form to get more information because they fear you'll spam them. Or, even worse, their phone will ring with a pushy salesperson on the other end.

One way to build trust is to use a series of small commitments that involve minimal risk to the customer. Each small "yes" makes the next one easier, creating psychological momentum toward the ultimate conversion.

For example, if your CTA is "Book a free consultation," you may find customers are reluctant to take that step. Will it be a helpful consultation, or a high-pressure sales pitch? Instead, structure a series of small commitments; for example:

- Click an article link (zero commitment)
- Read the article (time investment)
- Download a free guide (email given)
- Attend a webinar (calendar commitment)
- Book a consultation (the goal)

Each step builds trust through reciprocity and consistency. Try this prompt to get ideas for a sequence that will work for your situation:

```
You are an expert in commitment psychology and
trust building. Design a microcommitment
sequence that will encourage more customers to
```

```
[your goal, e.g., schedule a consultation].
Think about why customers may not do that now,
like fears, psychological barriers, process
friction, etc. Then, use your knowledge of our
customer profiles, brand, industry, etc. to
create five steps that gradually increase
commitment and build trust through reciprocity.
[Optional: Additional information—website URL,
available content and/or tools, etc.]
```

For example, given this prompt with only the goal ("book a free pool cleaning estimate") and a pool company's website URL, Gemini offered a handy sequence of increasing small commitments. It offered plenty of detail for each step, but here's a summary:

- Step 1: The "Pool Care Cheat Sheet"—offer a free PDF guide, "7 Secrets to a Sparkling Clean Pool." *Commitment: an email address.*

- Step 2: The "5-Minute Pool Health Check"—an interactive quiz that asks simple questions and gives a "Pool Health Score" with an explanation. *Commitment: a few minutes of time and basic pool info.*

- Step 3: The "Personalized Maintenance Plan"—offer a more detailed document with a suggested maintenance schedule and explanation. *Commitment: email confirmation and a few pool details.*

- Step 4: The "15-Minute Virtual Consultation"—offer a free, no-obligation 15-minute video call with a CPO-certified technician. No sales pitch, just friendly expert advice. *Commitment: schedule a specific time for the call.*

- Step 5: The "Free In-Person Estimate"—trust and credibility have been established, now it's time to ask for the original objective. *Commitment: schedule the in-person estimate.*

This might seem like overkill for a small business, but the series of small commitments will almost certainly lead to an increase in bookings. The booking option could be offered after each step, since in some cases the free pool care guide would be enough to create trust. Or, the customer might have an immediate need. A larger company could offer the virtual consultation step, but a smaller operation might go straight to the in-person estimate.

As with any prompt, follow-up questions can help. For example:

```
I like the idea of the Pool Cheat Sheet, can you
help me create it?
```

Or, here's another example:

```
We don't have the staff to do virtual
consultations, can we skip that step or do
something different?
```

Anti-Trust Signals: Find Your Credibility Killers

Sometimes the biggest trust gains come from removing trust killers. Vague, unattributed testimonials do more damage than good. Some issues are serious, like hidden costs that show up late in a process. Some, like using stock photos instead of actual shots of your people or customers, are more subtle. These anti-signals trigger skepticism faster than positive signals build confidence:

```
You are an expert in customer skepticism
and trust barriers. Use your knowledge of our
customer profiles, brand, industry, etc.
and audit this marketing for trust killers.
Include overpromising, inauthentic language,
questionable claims, missing information, lack
of professionalism in design or content, and
others. Rate each issue you find for importance
```

and provide fixes for each. *[Your website/ copy/offer]*

For example, on yet another pool maintenance site, Gemini detected multiple trust killers:

- Vague, unsubstantiated claims, e.g., "Best service in the area," and, "We guarantee the best service."
- Lack of social proof on key pages, including the home page.
- No pricing or process transparency.
- Use of stock images instead of actual techs or customers.
- An About Us page so wordy that most people won't read it.

Naturally, the AI suggested specific fixes for each problem.

Trust Transference Strategies

People transfer trust from entities they already trust to associated entities. This is related to but not exactly the same as authority. This psychological shortcut explains why celebrity endorsements work. Boxing legend George Foreman had no authority in the grilling or cooking space, but his fame and likable personality enabled him to sell millions of tabletop grills. And it's why "As seen on CNN" badges matter.

Chances are, if you've been lucky enough to have received positive coverage from a major media outlet, you are already leveraging that. AI can help you think of new ways to use trust transference.

Using your context knowledge, try this prompt. We're posing a wide ranging question with several moving parts. You can run it on your regular model, but deep research will yield better results:

> You are an expert in trust transference and association. Use your knowledge of my customer profiles, brand, industry, etc. and think about

immediate trust transfer opportunities, associations to build going forward, partnership possibilities, content collaboration, speaking at conferences, appearing on podcasts, etc. Consider what others in this industry have done. Then, suggest trust sources I can legitimately leverage and the best way to approach them.

Trust Transference Example

Running the prompt on Gemini Pro for a prominent local photographer's website produced a reasonable set of ideas. Some were straightforward, like showcasing testimonials, adding "behind the scenes" photos to show the process, adding "as seen on" references if any, etc. It suggested networking with businesses like wedding photographers, real estate companies, and interior designers. Other generic recommendations were guest blogging, Instagram takeovers, and "style shoots" with other vendors. Three conference and three podcast ideas were all photography themed. The AI offered a few tips for how to pitch event organizers and podcasters.

The recommendations were all solid, if a bit obvious.

Trust Transference Example with Deep Research

The identical prompt on Gemini Pro Deep Research produced markedly different results. The AI created a 20-page report that included an analysis of the competitive landscape, including profiles of three competitors. It identified local business associations that might provide partnership opportunities. Other categories were corporate events and co-working spaces. In each case, Gemini suggested the value the photographer could add and how the relationship could be leveraged for trust.

It even included a thought leadership strategy. This included a detailed implementation plan that started with quick wins and added activities that could continue for three years. This wasn't a plan ready to adopt without modification, but overall there was a high level of detail that included how-to details and expected trust signals. Even picking two or three of the dozens of ideas outlined could help the business boost trust and revenue.

The lesson: when you really want your AI to do the job of an expensive consultant, use the deep research version of the model. Don't blindly follow its recommendations, but use them as a rich source of ideas and starting points.

What's Next

In the next chapter, we'll explore decision architecture—how to structure choices so the right decision feels obvious. You'll learn why most pricing pages sabotage sales and how small changes in presentation can double conversion rates.

For updates and copy/paste prompt text visit rogerdooley.com/engine.

Chapter 12

Decision Architecture and Pricing

Every choice you present to customers is affected, often in a major way, by how you present it.

The human brain uses predictable shortcuts when evaluating options. The structure of those options can determine the outcome, often more than the options themselves. This chapter reveals how to create a decision architecture that guides customers toward choices that benefit both of you.

The Choice Paradox in Practice

You've probably heard of the paradox of choice. You know that too many options can paralyze decision-making. But knowing this and applying it effectively are two different things.

The paradox is less about absolute quantities and more about cognitive processing. Three options can cause customers to leave without acting if they're complex and unclear. Twenty options can feel simple if they're well-organized and clearly differentiated. Amazon has a seemingly infinite number of options but still thrives.

Try this prompt to diagnose choice overload in your offerings:

```
You are an expert in choice architecture and
decision psychology. Use your knowledge of our
customer profiles, brand, industry, etc. Analyze
our current options for cognitive overload.
Consider difficulty in comparison. Determine
```

```
which differences are important, where customers
might stall, and provide recommendations for
restructuring the choices. [Your options, e.g.,
URL for your pricing page]
```

Using Gemini Pro and this prompt on the pricing page of a popular CRM software found some good points, like highlighting the middle of five choices as "Most Popular." It found some flaws, too. One thing that would confuse customers were features present in the Basic and Pro plans but inexplicably absent in the Standard plan. Were they left off by mistake, or is the Standard plan less advanced than the cheaper one?

Another point of confusion was a huge variation in the number of "AI Credits" each plan had. A new customer would have difficulty evaluating how many they needed or what value the bigger numbers represented.

Gemini had a number of straightforward ideas to reduce confusion and cognitive load. The most obvious was to fix or clarify the missing features problem. It also suggested rather than enumerating all of the individual features they simplified into a "Workflow Power Pack" for the more expensive plan. Text could be added to the cryptic AI credit numbers to explain the use case, e.g., "for complex, multi-step workflows."

One recommendation I liked was to change the CTA for the unpriced Enterprise version from the intimidating, "Contact Sales," to a more friendly, "Learn More." That button would link to a page with more information on benefits, supportive case studies, and a CTA reading, "Request Demo." It also suggested a small "recommender" quiz titled "Find Your Plan" to help customers choose without having to research what AI credits were and sort out other confusing features.

Several of these improvements struck me as very solid quick wins. And the site Gemini analyzed wasn't a sketchy SaaS startup, the brand has more than $1 billion in annual revenue.

Gemini on Gemini

Just for fun, I ran the same prompt on Gemini's own pricing page, again using Gemini Pro. The response was, well, amusing. "The Gemini subscription page is a model of simplicity and a masterclass in reducing cognitive overload. Its choice architecture is exceptionally clean, presenting a clear, binary choice that is easy for users to process." Biased? You decide . . .

The Decoy Effect: Steering Preference

A decoy product is a powerful way for marketers to guide customers to a particular choice. Decoy products are ones that you don't expect to sell well, but as part of a set of choices nudge a customer to the one you hope to sell more of.

One kind of decoy is a product that isn't quite as good as your target product but is priced the same or close to it. The similarities between the prices make the better product seem more attractive than if it was presented alone. Nobody will buy the decoy, but you'll sell more of the target product.

Another decoy can be a high-priced, top of the line product. Add this costly choice to your mix, and the product that was previously the most expensive now seems like a compromise, a middle-of-the-road choice. You may sell few or none of the high-end product, but you'll sell more of the less expensive one. When a third choice is added to two existing ones, you get the classic "Good, Better, Best" model.

Decoy products can work in anything from SaaS products to appliances. Want to check your lineup for a decoy strategy? Try this prompt:

```
You are a behavioral economist with deep
knowledge of the decoy effect and using decoy
products to increase sales. Review our current
product/pricing and suggest possible decoy
strategies. [your product/pricing info; the
specific product you want to boost].
```

For example, Gemini Pro analyzed the pricing page of a popular online graphics editor. For individuals, there are only two options—Free and Pro. An unpriced Enterprise version has a "Contact Sales" CTA. The company would clearly prefer Pro users to free ones. To make the Pro option more enticing, Gemini suggested a new decoy level, "Pro Lite," priced just 20% less than Pro but with fewer features and some limits on usage. Few or no customers would buy the Pro Lite plan, but sales of Pro should increase. Classic use of a decoy product.

Default Power: Frictionless Choice

Defaults are decisions made without deciding. They're powerful because they work with our brain, trying to conserve mental energy whenever possible. Deciding between more than one choice needs System 2, that uncomfortable, logical process. Doing nothing is pure System 1.

This simple approach is why when signing up for a retirement plan is the default—no form to complete, the employee is automatically opted in—far more employees participate. (They are free to opt out, of course.) Vastly more drivers agree to donate organs if they are opted in when getting their license than if they must manually sign up.

There are simple ways to use this. Making one choice far more obvious than the rest, highlighting it as "Most Common," and similar methods imply that's the default. A true use of default would be to have several options with check boxes with the one you think is best for the customer already checked. The customer doesn't need to decide, only to click "Next."

You may be able to sort this out without your AI consultant, but if you want advice, give this a try:

> You are an expert in default bias and choice architecture. Use your knowledge of our customer profiles, brand, industry, etc. and analyze our current decision process. Suggest any ethical

> way or ways to use a default choice to improve
> sales or customer outcomes. [Your pricing or
> product page, or other set of choices.]

For example, Gemini Pro analyzed a five-choice SaaS pricing page and came up with a few ideas. Setting a "smart default" based on the customer profile (number of users) was one idea. Preselecting the preferred option during onboarding (without hiding the others) was another.

Using a model in agent mode that could actually make selections, click buttons, etc., might produce additional insights.

Anchoring in Action

The first number customers see becomes their reference point for all subsequent numbers. This anchoring effect is so powerful it works even when the anchor number is irrelevant. Equally surprising is that the individual is unaware of this effect. Dan Ariely's classic experiment primed subjects with a number from 0 to 99 (the anchor) and asked them to estimate the price of an unfamiliar product. The higher the anchor, the more likely subjects were to assign a higher price to the product.[1]

Most businesses make anchoring mistakes. The majority of SaaS pricing pages I encounter lead with the cheapest plan and finish with the most expensive. Anchoring research shows that showing people a higher price first makes the subsequent lower prices seem even more like a bargain.

When an infomercial or video ad leads with, "Thousands sold at $399!" they are setting the anchor. The real price of $199, revealed later, will seem like a steal.

Try this prompt on your website or other marketing material:

> You are an expert in price anchoring and
> reference point psychology. Use your knowledge
> of our customer profiles, brand, industry, etc.

```
and create an anchoring strategy that will
maximize sales. If relevant, think about the
optimal number to show first and any revelation
sequence. Consider non-price anchors and
comparisons to higher-priced options from
others or alternative products/services. [your
product/service, actual price(s)]
```

Example: Pricing Page with Five Choices

From this simple prompt referencing a SaaS pricing page with five choices, ranging from "Free" to "Enterprise," both Gemini Pro and ChatGPT 5 came up with the same primary idea: completely flip the order so that Enterprise was the first thing people would see. And both thought adding a number, for example "Starting at $15,000," to the currently unpriced Enterprise would make it a more powerful anchor. Both had other suggestions for improvement that weren't pure anchoring strategies.

Example: Single Product

A SaaS pricing page is a straightforward challenge, but could AI come up with something creative for a service with just one price? Running the same prompt with, "I am a photographer that specializes in business headshots for $599 per session," produced interesting results.

Gemini Pro didn't hesitate to suggest that the single price was a mistake. Instead, the photographer should lead with a $1,299 Executive Package that would serve as both a decoy product and a high anchor that would make the $599 price, now renamed the Professional Package, seem like a great value. A $349 Starter Package would be very limited to make the $599 deal the logical way to go. To enhance the anchor power, Gemini suggested, the $1,299 package should be the only one visible before revealing the less expensive ones.

ChatGPT 5 came up with a roughly similar strategy. Lead with a Premium Executive Session for $1,995, keep the current Business Headshot Session at $599, and offer a minimal LinkedIn Express Headshot for $299. Naturally, the $599 offer would be revealed only after customers had been exposed to the much more costly package.

Both models offered additional suggestions for different anchors. One example was, "Top corporate photographers in NYC charge $1,500–$3,000 for a similar session." (I'd check something like that for accuracy before putting it in my marketing, but the concept is good.) Another suggested a non-price anchor, pointing out that a bad first impression from a LinkedIn profile photo could be costly in lost sales leads or a missed job offer.

Loss Framing vs. Gain Framing

When is a number not the same number? It's when the number is presented as a gain vs. a loss. Loss aversion means people feel losses twice as powerfully as equivalent gains. But context determines which frame works better.

Products and services can often be characterized as prevention focused or promotion focused. Prevention products include things like burglar alarms, insurance, and routine maintenance. All of these prevent losses but offer few gains. Promotion-oriented products are gain focused. These are things like vacation travel, investments, and training.

Products can sometimes be presented in either way. A conservative mutual fund could be sold as a way to build wealth (promotion) or to minimize losses during downturns (prevention). Training could be offered as a way to avoid career disaster or to open up exciting new opportunities. Confusingly, perhaps, individual people may have prevention or promotion mindsets.

Want AI to help you weigh the pros and cons of each approach and help you create effective messaging? Try this prompt:

```
You are an expert in message framing and
prevention vs. promotion focuses and mindsets.
Use your knowledge of our customer profiles,
brand, industry, etc. to analyze our marketing
and suggest the best framing options, including
specific language and test recommendations for:
[your product/service, your website, etc.]
```

For example, ChatGPT 5 analyzed a small business security software website using this prompt and found it was mostly prevention-oriented by focusing on topics like loss of data and business disruption. The AI recommended a mixed framing strategy for maximum impact, i.e., combining both prevention and promotion messaging. But it also provided alternate messaging that was oriented to either loss or gain, and created a testing protocol to evaluate all three approaches. It offered additional messaging for things like call-out boxes and suggested specific types of messaging for different customer groups.

Temporal Framing: "When" Beats "What"

The same offer feels different depending on temporal framing. For example, "$1,200/year" feels expensive, but "$100/month" feels manageable. "$3.29/day" feels cheap, and "Less than a coffee per day" puts that minimal cost into perspective.

If you are selling subscriptions or any type of product or service with recurring billing, AI can help you reframe the amount you charge every month into something more appealing to your customers. Even infrequently purchased products can be reframed in this way. Try this prompt:

> You are an expert in temporal reframing and pricing psychology. Use your knowledge of our customer profiles, brand, industry, etc. and suggest ways to optimize the time framing. Consider the main temporal frame, supporting comparisons, and ways to align time and value.
> [your pricing, your website, etc.]

For example, using that prompt, Gemini Pro looked at a business security software site and thought that their sole pricing display of an annual cost was probably costing them sales. Merely expressing it as a low monthly cost would help. It suggested two other copy changes that would also use temporal framing: highlighting the daily cost in cents and using terms like "24/7 protection" and "around the clock" to put the actual cost in the best possible light.

Choice Architecture and Pricing Psychology Audit

In this chapter, we've focused on many individual strategies. But, what if you don't know where to begin? Or maybe you just want a quick win or two. A deep research or agent prompt may be just what you need to get started.

A word of caution, though . . . the more general the assignment, the more your AI is likely to miss things. A good example comes from SaaS pricing page analysis. It took asking the AI models to specifically think about anchoring before they suggested reversing the order to put the most expensive ones first. Despite price anchoring being a fundamental strategy, all of the previous analyses ignored that as an intervention. So, with that warning, feel free to try this using a deep research or agent tool:

> You are an expert in behavioral science and consumer psychology. You are tasked with

conducting a deep analysis of the website listed at the end. Identify opportunities for improvement based on established principles of choice architecture, decision architecture, and pricing psychology. Create a structured report that includes a summary of the website's existing strategies in each area and a detailed list of specific, evidence-based interventions to test.

You must consider, but are not limited to, the following concepts:

Choice & Decision Architecture: defaults, framing, decoy effect, choice overload, friction in the user journey

Pricing Psychology: anchoring, temporal reframing, bundling/unbundling, loss vs. gain framing

Provide clear rationale for each recommendation, citing the specific psychological principle it leverages. List the recommendations in order of expected impact and highlight any easy-to-implement quick wins. [Website URL]

What's Next

Next up: scarcity and urgency, two of the most powerful psychological triggers in marketing, and two of the most frequently misused. We'll explore why "limited time offers" create such strong reactions in our brains, and when countdown timers actually boost conversions versus when they just annoy customers. You'll discover how smart brands create genuine urgency without resorting to the fake "Almost gone!" tactics that erode trust.

For updates and copy/paste prompt text visit rogerdooley.com/engine.

Chapter 13

Scarcity, Urgency, and FOMO

"Only 3 left in stock!"
"Sale ends in 2 hours!"
"Limited-time offer!"

Why do you see these messages everywhere? Quite simply, because they work. But they have a dark side, too. This chapter reveals the psychology behind scarcity, urgency, and the Fear of Missing Out (FOMO), and how to use them ethically for sustainable results.

The Psychology of Scarcity

Scarcity isn't a gimmick, even if some marketers treat it like one. Scarcity is a fundamental psychological trigger that evolved to help humans survive. When resources appear limited, our brains shift into acquisition mode. Our instinctive response can overwhelm logical evaluation and trigger immediate action. Remember when you reflexively hit the "Buy with 1-Click" button on Amazon because there was only one left in stock and you were afraid you'd lose it?

Scarcity is such a powerful trigger because it comes from multiple mechanisms:

- Loss aversion: We fear missing out on something.
- Increased valuation: Scarce things seem more desirable.
- Social proof: Others want it, it must be good.
- Reactance: Scarcity threatens our freedom of choice.

Each of these mechanisms may be more important for a particular marketing situation, but they work in concert to move customers to act.

Scarcity's Dark Side

Because of its power, scarcity is one of the most commonly misused and abused influence principles. Fake scarcity is everywhere. Think of the sketchy big city stores that had "going out of business" sales every few weeks. Or, the "Only 1 room left" hotel listing that was still there on the website, even after you supposedly booked the last one.

I was once duped into a hasty purchase by a website with a giant sale that expired at midnight that same day. The prices were great and a big countdown timer showed how little time was left to take advantage of them. Not wanting to miss out, I dumped the items I wanted into my cart and sped through the checkout process. When I returned the next day to check on my order, I was surprised to find the same giant sale, once again ending at midnight. Unsurprisingly, it was there the day after that, too. I felt a bit foolish for my haste in ordering, but the experience was a valuable lesson in the power of time-driven scarcity. Even fake scarcity.

Scarcity in marketing can backfire in several ways. Fake scarcity destroys trust. I had always held a positive impression of the brand behind the endless "ends at midnight" sale, but that one experience showed me the firm's true character. Heavy scarcity users like travel booking sites have devised workarounds to allow their "one room left" messaging to stay within the law, but overuse can reduce both the credibility and impact of the messages.

The power of scarcity to drive quick, instinctive purchases can in some cases lead to reduced customer satisfaction and higher return rates on physical products.

Scarcity is powerful—use it wisely and ethically.

Find Your Scarcity

If you are thinking that scarcity won't work because whatever you are offering isn't scarce, don't write off the approach just yet. There are ethical ways to invoke scarcity even when there's no shortage. Try this prompt:

```
You are an expert in scarcity psychology and
consumer behavior. Use your knowledge of our
customer profiles, brand, industry, etc. to
suggest ways to use scarcity to increase sales.
Consider which scarcity mechanisms will be most
effective and how to frame the scarcity in a
powerful but ethical way. Warn of any possible
ways these ideas could backfire. Rate each idea
for its expected positive impact on sales.
[your offer, your website, etc.].
```

Example: Ad Agency

Even though there are real limits imposed by team size and scalability, it's not common to see ad agencies using scarcity to market themselves. They tend to focus on their client brands, their creative portfolio, awards they've won, success stories, team qualifications, etc. Claude Opus 4 executed this prompt on a small marketing agency's website and came up with eight different ways to use scarcity. I've summarized a few:

- Team Bandwidth Transparency (Impact 9/10)—messaging like, "Current availability: Web Development (booking into March), Brand Strategy (2 weeks out)."

- Founding Team Access Scarcity (9/10)—"Jeff Jones (Founder) personally leads only 5 strategic projects per year. Apply for consideration."

- Early-Bird MSAP (Marketing Strategy Action Plan) Pricing (7/10)— "Book your MSAP consultation by [date] and lock in current year pricing before our annual rate increase."

- Limited-Time Strategic Audits (8/10)—"Complimentary brand audits available for the next 10 businesses only—normally $2,500 value."

All of the other ideas were at least plausible. Claude, of course, had no internal details to work with. Maybe Jeff (not the real name) spends most of his time on his sailboat these days. Maybe all the teams have bandwidth right now—good for new clients, but not for honest scarcity. Still, I can imagine the agency scanning the list and saying, "This one's pretty good, let's try it next time we're in business development mode."

Example—Luggage Brand

The identical prompt on ChatGPT 5 for an established but low-key luxury luggage brand website produced ideas like the ones summarized here:

- Limited-Quantity Drops (High impact)—release small batches of exclusive colors or features.
- Time-Limited Offers (High)—flash sales (e.g., "48-hour free monogramming") or offers that expire soon.
- Seasonal & Limited-Edition Collections (Moderate to High)—seasonal colors or design collaborations only available for a limited time.
- "Only X Left in Stock" Messaging (Moderate)—Show low remaining inventory counts on product pages, must be accurate.
- Early Access for VIPs or Loyalty Members (Moderate)—Let loyalty members view or pre-order new releases early.

The psychology behind each was explained. The AI understood the brand's image well enough to share plenty of cautions both on the individual ideas and at the end. It warned the brand should never fake scarcity and not overuse scarcity to avoid desensitizing customers. Selective use of scarcity can enhance a luxury brand's image, but overuse can damage it.

Authentic vs. Artificial Scarcity

The internet has a way of exposing fake scarcity. Customers screenshot fake countdown timers that reset. They notice when "only 2 left" never changes, even after a purchase. When they share these discoveries, brand trust and reputation are damaged.

Authentic scarcity comes from real constraints:

- Physical inventory limitations
- Time-bound opportunities
- Capacity restrictions
- Exclusive access rights
- Seasonal availability

If you are using scarcity triggers that make you feel a bit queasy, run this prompt:

> You are an expert in ethical persuasion and trust. Transform our current scarcity into authentic scarcity. Do it in a way that is clear, authentic, and helpful, not manipulative. Suggest five options and rate them for positive impact. *[your current offer using scarcity]*

Example—Digital Course. Claude Opus 4 executed the prompt with the appended information, "We sell a digital course, 'Creating Viral Videos with AI,' for $99. There are no limits on availability, but our previous marketing manager added a message, 'Only 3 spots left!' next to the price." The ideas Claude came up with included:

- Time-Sensitive Pricing Transparency—"Current price: $99 (increasing to $129 on [specific date] as we add new modules"
- Bonus Resource Scarcity—"Enroll today and receive 1-on-1 AI prompt optimization session (next 20 students only—12 remaining)"
- Cohort-Based Learning Windows—"Join our January cohort starting Monday—next group begins February 3rd"
- Founding Member Benefits—"Become one of our first 100 founding members: lifetime updates + exclusive community access"

Claude explained each one and recommended combining the first two for best results. The AI emphasized that the pricing, offer capacity limits, etc., must all be truthful.

Urgency Without Anxiety

Urgency is usually discussed as a way of invoking scarcity based on time, not quantity. The problem with many urgency tactics is that they can create anxiety rather than motivation. Aggressive countdown timers, flashing warnings, and pushy language activate a reactance response that can paralyze instead of persuade.

Have you ever had a salesperson present you with an ultimatum like, "You have to decide now, the offer expires today," and glare at you expectantly? Your first instinct would likely be to say, "Fine, I decided, we're done here." Bad urgency marketing can make customers react the same way.

Properly crafted urgency provides the customer with reasons to act now but doesn't induce panic. Try this prompt:

> You are an expert in temporal psychology, decision momentum, and influence principles. Use your knowledge of our customer profiles, brand, industry, etc. to create urgency messages that motivate without causing anxiety. Focus on customer benefits, explain the reasoning behind any deadlines, and use a calm, helpful tone. Offer a safety valve for hesitant buyers. Create five ideas and rate them for impact. *[your offer, your website, etc.,—include any real deadlines]*

For example, after analyzing a landscaping company's website, Gemini Pro suggested some low-stress ways to invoke urgency. One example: "The Early Bird Design Plan," that came with the message, "Dreaming of a new landscape for next spring? Let's start planning now. Our design schedule for spring installations fills up by late winter. By beginning the design process this fall, you get our undivided attention . . ." The safety valve was a no-obligation design consultation. All five of Gemini's suggestions gave a reason to act during a specific time frame but nudged the customer gently.

Without the prompt for low anxiety, we might have seen messaging like, "Don't miss the spring planting window, call today to avoid an ugly yard this summer!"

The Scarcity Spectrum

Not all scarcity is created equal. Different types activate different psychological responses:

- Quantity Scarcity, like "Only 10 left," triggers loss aversion and is best for physical products and exclusive items/offers.
- Time Scarcity, like "Sale ends Saturday," triggers urgency and FOMO and works for promotions and launches.

- Access Scarcity, like "By invitation only," triggers status seeking and belonging and works well for premium offerings and communities.
- Bonus Scarcity, like "First 50 subscribers get . . ." appeals to reward seeking and is good for launches and situations that need an initial boost.

Marketers can think of ways to apply any or all of these to a given scenario. What's the best choice for your situation? Run this prompt:

```
You are an expert in influence marketing and
using all types of scarcity. Use your knowledge
of our customer profiles, brand, industry, etc.
to determine the type or types of scarcity that
will work best. Consider using quantity, time,
limited access, and other scarcity types. Explain
your choices and suggest detailed messaging.
[your offer, your website, etc.]
```

For example, Gemini Pro executed this prompt on a cosmetic dentistry website. After determining that the dentists were positioning their service as a high-end offering, it recommended two types of scarcity. The first was "expertise scarcity," focusing on the unique credentials and experience of the providers to add authority and create urgency. If the patient believes there are very few providers at this level of expertise in the entire area, they will act quickly to secure an appointment.

The second was the more familiar access scarcity. By contrasting the limited amount of expert provider time with descriptions of an unrushed patient experience, it follows that only a small number of patients will be able to benefit. This, too, encourages booking sooner to avoid missing out.

Gemini provided the reasoning behind the choices and gave implementation instructions.

Power Up Scarcity with Social Proof

Scarcity becomes exponentially more powerful when combined with social proof. Say you're searching for a hotel for an upcoming conference. You find one within your budget that's close to the conference site. You see, "Only one room left at this price!" You consider grabbing it but see a few others that might be worth checking out. Then, the booking site pops up a message, "12 others viewing this hotel now!" Unconsciously, you think, "Hmm, others are interested, this one might be good." You also get an urgency trigger—one of those others might grab that last room. (You likely don't pause to calculate the very low probability that of all possible dates, those other guests want that same room on the same day.)

You are deciding whether to at least peek at the other nearby hotels when another message appears. "27 travelers like you booked this hotel in the last 48 hours!" This is a major blast of social proof—your fellow travelers aren't just shopping around, they're picking this exact hotel! Urgency ratchets up a bit more, too . . . You don't want to miss out on such a popular choice. So, you click the "Book now" button. If you could see them, the behavioral science team that designed these nudges would be high-fiving as you checked out.

Most of us don't want our websites or apps to be as cluttered with over-the-top, aggressive influence triggers, but we should consider adding social proof to make scarcity even more effective. Try this prompt:

```
You are an expert in scarcity psychology and
using influence principles to guide customer
behavior. Use your knowledge of our customers,
brand, industry, etc. to increase the power of
our scarcity messaging by adding social proof.
Consider how this might change, if at all,
during periods of high and low activity and
non-quantitative messaging that could be used.
```

```
Here is what we are doing now: [your website,
ad copy, etc.]
```

Using this prompt on an athletic footwear site, Gemini Pro came up with a range of ideas. A few were built around unique "drops"—scarce products in high demand. For more typical products, Gemini suggested typical scarcity cues like "Only 5 pair left in this size," combined with dynamic social proof, as in, "Over 500 people have purchased this in the last 24 hours."

The AI also provided some suggestions for slow periods or if dynamic data wasn't available. These ideas included evergreen social proof messages like, "A Member Favorite with 5,000+ 5-star reviews."

Ethical Scarcity

Scarcity, urgency, and FOMO are powerful motivators of customer behavior. Any kind of business, even those with no obvious limits on product or service availability, can use them by employing the techniques we've discussed. But, don't fall into the false scarcity trap. Be a scarcity user, not abuser.

What's Next

In the next chapter, we'll move beyond individual techniques into advanced AI behavioral strategies. We'll explore how to assemble virtual panels of behavioral science experts that debate and refine your approach, apply persuasion principles to complex B2B decisions with multiple stakeholders, and use AI to discover and understand the psychological tactics your competitors are already using. These are the techniques that separate marketers who dabble in behavioral science from those who build it into everything they do and make it their unfair advantage.

For updates and copy/paste prompt text visit rogerdooley.com/engine.

Chapter 14

Advanced AI Behavioral Techniques

You've been using AI to apply individual behavioral principles. You've learned to combine them effectively. Now it's time to unlock AI's full potential for behavioral marketing—techniques so powerful they'll transform how you understand and influence customer behavior.

This chapter shows you advanced AI strategies that produce results like those that marketing consultancies charge six figures to deploy. You'll learn to convene expert panels that debate your challenges, map invisible psychological journeys, predict behavioral responses before launching campaigns, and build systems that get smarter with every interaction.

Multi-Expert Panels: Beyond Single Perspectives

When facing complex marketing challenges, why settle for one expert's view? AI lets you assemble dream teams of behavioral scientists, marketers, and industry leaders. We've occasionally sprinkled expert names in some of our prompts, sometimes more than one. But, what if instead of merely priming the AI model with their ideas, the experts were debating your specific challenge? The magic happens when these perspectives clash, merge, and synthesize into insights no single expert could provide.

This prompt will convene your expert panel:

```
You are facilitating a behavioral marketing
expert panel consisting of: Robert Cialdini
(influence principles); Daniel Kahneman
(cognitive biases); BJ Fogg (behavior design);
Seth Godin (modern marketing); Jeff Bezos
(entrepreneurship, growth, leadership)
   Each expert should:

1. Provide their unique perspective on the
   problem
2. Suggest solutions from their framework
3. Respectfully challenge other experts' ideas
4. Build on others' suggestions

   After individual perspectives, the panel
should synthesize recommendations into a
unified strategy that combines the best insights.
   Use your knowledge of our customer profiles,
brand, industry, etc., to inform the results.
Here's the challenge: [Your challenge description]
```

For example, Gemini Pro ran this interesting prompt using the URL of a major SaaS website. The challenge was to create a plan to increase the number of signups for either free or paid plans. The panelists began by offering their perspectives, in some cases applying those to specific website messaging or features.

These comments offered useful insights even before the discussion. Even the expected ones, like Cialdini suggesting adding authority, social proof, and scarcity, included specific details like swapping the bland "Get Started" CTA to "Sign up this week and get a free one-on-one onboarding session." Godin also took issue with "Get Started," saying that would be too big a step for many visitors. He suggested offering them a high-value piece of content for their email address. Bezos thought an AI-powered chat feature on the homepage that can answer questions 24/7 would be much more helpful than the existing "Contact Sales" link.

Next, each expert offered a sentence or two during the synthesis phase. This seemed a bit perfunctory and unhelpful, but the final recommendations reflected deeper thought. These ideas included:

- Homepage "Wizard" and Personalization: A short quiz to segment users and deliver the most relevant case studies, etc.
- Radically Simplify Sign-Up and Onboarding: Use one-click sign-up with Google/Microsoft (credited to Fogg rather than one-click pioneer Bezos); immediately help on-board the user with a pre-built template.
- Amplify Social Proof and Authority: Replace static logos with dynamic, targeted short video testimonials; add "As Seen In" logos from top publications.
- Embrace a "Day 1" Testing Culture: Aggressively A/B test all key elements: headlines, calls to action; test "loss aversion" messaging against the current "gain" messaging; test bold, "Purple Cow" headlines. (Guess who suggested that one?)
- Build a Permission-Based Funnel: Offer a high-value download (e.g., an e-book or template pack) in exchange for their email. Nurture these leads with targeted content.

Are these the five best possible interventions? I doubt it. But both the recommendations and prior discussion offer ideas from different schools of thought. Some could be a starting point for a deeper dive into optimizing, for example, a CTA.

Novelty is the goal. Had we posed the challenge to an AI model without the panel approach, there's zero chance it would have come up with Purple Cow headlines or a permission marketing approach.

Use a panel like this as a starting point, not the final word. Shake up the group with some non-obvious choices like an industry expert or business coach. Whoever said, "There are no bad ideas" was wrong. There are lots of bad ideas everywhere. Run this prompt, ignore the bad ones, and find a few good ones.

Food Fight: Make Your Experts Disagree

I've been in plenty of real-life meetings where great ideas emerge when individuals or factions disagree. So, force your AI experts to challenge each other; you never know what will happen. Here's a prompt to do that:

> You are moderating a heated but respectful debate between [your first expert] and [your second expert] about [your marketing strategy]. They have opposing views on whether to use [Approach 1] or [Approach 2].
> Structure:
>
> 1. Expert A makes their case (2-3 key points)
> 2. Expert B counters and presents alternative
> 3. Expert A responds to criticisms
> 4. Expert B addresses A's points
> 5. Find common ground
> 6. Synthesize a hybrid approach
>
> Keep exchanges sharp but professional. Each expert should cite research or examples supporting their position.

Running this prompt on Gemini Pro and ChatGPT 5 on a SaaS pricing page produced different opening arguments. Gemini had Ariely using an anchoring argument for showing the highest prices first.

ChatGPT had Thaler take that position. As with the previous prompt, the biggest value was the discussion. Each supported their approach with multiple research-based arguments helpful to a science-oriented marketer working on an issue like this.

The compromise recommendations were interesting but felt a bit forced. On Gemini, the experts decided on a highest-first approach but de-emphasizing the cheapest plan. ChatGPT found agreement by letting them both win: determine the size of their company first, then show small customers low prices first and enterprise buyers the opposite.

The real value in requiring agreement at the end is that it forces the AI to think of something new instead of regurgitating standard concepts like anchoring. Sometimes, the hybrid will be useless muddle, but there's also the chance for something novel. Repeating with a few different experts might actually yield a creative new approach.

Mobile-Specific Behavioral Psychology

Mobile screens are a fundamentally different psychological context than desktops. Thumb reach affects decision-making. People expect quicker results. Context switching is more difficult.

Mobile also presents challenges to AI analysis. ChatGPT doesn't have an iPhone, at least not yet. Just getting your mobile content and user experience into your AI model takes some effort. At the moment, capturing a screen video or a series of screenshots is the best option. If you're evaluating an interaction, you'll have to add an explanation of what you are doing and why. This is all far more effort than asking a model to check out a website where it can load pages, detect and visit links, and even (in some cases, like ChatGPT agent) interact. (AI models can interact with mobile websites, but the experience may not duplicate the smartphone experience.)

With those caveats, here's a prompt to optimize for mobile:

> You are a mobile behavioral psychology expert and mobile app developer who understands how device constraints and usage patterns create unique psychological states. Analyze these [screenshots/video] for mobile optimization.
>
> In evaluating this mobile app experience, assess how thumb reach and decision architecture influence action, how well it supports micro-moment psychology, the cognitive load imposed by small-screen constraints, and the impact of the user's context and environment on task completion.
>
> Provide specific adaptations that work with mobile psychology.
>
> This is the problem/question [what you are trying to optimize].

B2B Behavioral Differences

The biggest mistake marketers make about business buyers is thinking that they make decisions based on logic, unlike foolish B2C customers. To be sure, there are rational/logical elements that are part of B2B sales. A consumer can buy an iPhone on a whim, but most B2B purchases have to meet specific criteria for performance, price, delivery, etc.

Still, B2B buyers are humans and their choices often driven by biases and emotion. How will a buyer be judged if the ERP software they bought saves millions of dollars? Or, if it turns into a costly fiasco? How do they feel about the salesperson? The brand? Did one seller help them in a crunch situation the year before? There's more than logic involved.

If you sell to B2B buyers, adapt your prompts accordingly:

> You are a B2B behavioral psychology specialist who understands how organizational dynamics

> change individual psychology. Analyze this B2C principle [principle or bias name] and adapt it for B2B, factoring career risk and reputation, multi-stakeholder consensus, long decision cycles, demand for proof/ROI, and procurement hurdles.
>
> Provide specific B2B adaptations with examples.

For example, prompted to adapt Urgency/FOMO to a B2B mindset, Claude Opus 4.1 created a comprehensive report with five detailed examples plus several discussions of topics like multi-stakeholder urgency and long-cycle urgency. One example was "Competitive Intelligence Urgency," which instead of "only 3 left" used language that implied, "Your competitors are already using this and reducing operating costs by 20%."

Another example used "falling behind professionally" as B2B FOMO.

You can, of course, add your own knowledge context to get more specific advice.

Fear as a B2B Motivator

B2B decisions are driven by fear more than desire. As sales expert Matt Dixon told me, "FOMO doesn't drive B2B buyers, it's FOMU." He explained that FOMU is Fear of Messing Up. A bad decision by a buyer can derail their career. Use this prompt to uncover your buyer's hidden fears:

> You are an expert in organizational psychology and B2B sales, skilled in analyzing unconscious fears in B2B buying decisions. Using your

```
knowledge of our customer profiles, brand,
industry, etc., identify:

1. Career fears (what could go wrong for them
   personally)
2. Team fears (disruption, rebellion, competence)
3. Organizational      fears      (reputation,
   competitiveness)
4. Implementation fears (technical, cultural,
   financial)

   Then suggest how to address each fear without
triggering defensive responses. [Optional—add
your context to focus the response]
```

For example, Claude Opus 4.1 examined the website of a large industrial lubricant supplier using this prompt to develop a detailed list of fear examples in each of the four categories. It broke them down into technical, cultural, and financial anxieties and offered ways to address those fears without triggering defensiveness. It concluded with a handful of recommended communication strategies like these two:

- Instead of saying: "Your current lubricant is inferior," say: "You've maximized what your current solution can deliver."
- Instead of saying: "You need to modernize," say: "You're ready for the next level of performance."

Competitive Behavioral Analysis

Your competitors' behavioral tactics reveal what works in your market and what customers have been trained to expect. This advanced prompt creates a behavioral intelligence report and will work best in deep research mode:

You are a competitive intelligence analyst with deep knowledge of behavioral science and persuasion psychology. Examine these competitors: *[URLs or marketing materials]*. Then, create a comprehensive report analyzing:

1. Behavioral Principles Inventory
   - Which principles they use
   - How sophisticated their implementation is
   - What's working (based on their continued use)
2. Customer Psychology Training
   - What behaviors they've normalized
   - Expectations they've created
   - Trust signals customers now expect or require
3. Gaps and Opportunities
   - Principles they're missing
   - Poor implementations to improve upon
   - Over-used tactics creating fatigue
4. Strategic Recommendations

   Use your knowledge of our customer profiles, brand, etc., to suggest
   - Which successful tactics to adopt (but improve)
   - Which gaps to exploit
   - How to differentiate behaviorally

In research mode, Claude Opus 4.1 created an 8-page report on three SaaS companies' CRM software websites. There were plenty of insights to work with. A few highlights:

- All were using social proof heavily, albeit in different ways. Examples were detailed for each competitor, including language like, "73,000 businesses." Some added success metrics, like "100% pipeline growth" or "40% cost reduction."
- Use of authority varied. One firm displayed 15 different certifications. In contrast, another mentioned a couple of certifications in the text but displayed no trust symbols at all.
- All competitors invoked reciprocity with risk-free trials. Claude concluded that customers have been conditioned to expect multi-week trials with no credit card required.
- A missing trigger on all competitor websites was urgency/scarcity. Claude recommended implementing dynamic urgency messaging for monthly cohort limits, time-decaying discounts or specials, etc.
- All competitors were using gain-based messaging. The AI suggested that loss-prevention messaging might drive more business, like, "Stop bleeding $50,000 monthly from pipeline leakage."
- One intriguing idea was to position the company running the study as "The Behavioral CRM,"—software that "doesn't just track customer behavior but actively shapes it through integrated behavioral science."

There were many additional competitive insights and suggested strategies, some more practical than others. Overall, the competitive insights seemed on point and at least a few of the recommendations could be starting points for further research.

I'd recommend creating a deep-dive competition research report like this, saving it, and making it part of your knowledge. Add it to the projects or custom GPTs you use for science-based persuasion. When you run prompts like those covered in preceding chapters, your AI won't be recommending strategies or messaging in a vacuum. Instead, it will know the competitive landscape.

Building Your Behavioral Prompt Library

Your prompts are valuable intellectual property. The best ones, refined through use, become competitive advantages. Don't lose your prompts, or key information on what worked and what didn't!

Your system could be as simple as a cloud document where you paste your best prompts, revising as you find ways to improve their output. If you want something more sophisticated that helps you track performance, here's a prompt to get you started:

```
You are an expert in behavioral science and
prompt engineering.
   Create a simple, usable Behavioral Prompt
Library that helps a marketer or small team
store, organize, and improve their best prompts.
   Include:
   Categories—organized by behavioral principle
(e.g., scarcity, social proof), application
(e.g., email, landing page), and industry/context.
   Prompt Templates—reusable core structures
with [brackets] for customization, clear context
requirements, and expected output formats.
   Improvement Tracking—an easy way to record
versions, results, and lessons learned from
successes and failures.
```

```
   Usage Tips—guidance on when to use each prompt,
how to customize, and how to interpret results.
   Output in a table format that can be copied
and pasted into Excel or Google Sheets. Populate
with example entries for at least two behavioral
principles.
```

Edit the prompt as necessary to match your needs. Or, run it and edit the columns after you paste it into your spreadsheet software. Because this prompt is fairly open-ended, your results may vary with the model and any additional info in your prompt. Gemini 2.5 Flash produced a simple, four-column sheet. ChatGPT 5's table had 6 columns. Claude Opus 4.1 produced a far more complex table with 13 columns to hold version numbering, results details, etc.

Spreadsheets aren't ideal for large text blocks like detailed prompts, but they do offer an easy way to organize and include other data like test results.

The marketers who win in the AI age will be the ones who build the best systems for generating, testing, and learning from behavioral interventions.

Wrapping Up Part 3

You now possess tools that would have seemed like magic just years ago. You can summon panels of world-class experts, predict customer psychology, and optimize for behaviors below their conscious awareness. And you can do this in minutes.

The companies dominating their markets five years from now will be those that started building their persuasive AI capabilities today. You've got the knowledge. You've got the tools. The only remaining question is: What will you optimize first?

Remember: With great power comes great responsibility. Trite, but true. Use these advanced techniques to help customers make decisions they'll thank you for, not to manipulate them into choices they'll regret. The best persuasive marketing creates value for everyone: customers, companies, and the larger community.

What's Next

In Part 4, we'll look at what many thought was a chasm AI could never cross: understanding human emotion and communicating with empathy.

It turns out many humans aren't very good at empathy and emotion, even CEOs and CMOs. Not a week goes by without a company being unpleasantly surprised when a policy change or important announcement gets unexpected blowback from customers, other stakeholders, or even the general public.

You'll learn how to use AI to audit both important and routine communications for empathy and predict the emotional reactions of the humans on the receiving end. You'll see how AI can help you craft messages that not only avoid tone-deaf gaffes but land with the desired emotional impact.

Believe it or not, AI will help you add the human touch.

For updates and copy/paste prompt text visit rogerdooley.com/engine.

Part IV

Empathy, Emotion, and Communication

"If there is any one secret of success, it lies in the ability to get the other person's point of view and see things from his angle as well as your own."

—Henry Ford

Part IV

Empathy, Emotion, and Communication

Chapter 15

AI Adds the Human Touch

Since the earliest days of computing, it was a given that computers were good at math but would never understand human emotion. "Robotic" was an adjective that, applied to a human, implied mechanical behavior devoid of emotion.

In 2021, researchers from San Francisco State University and Berkeley published a paper that declared empathetic AI to be, "impossible, immoral, or both."[1] As recently as 2023, AI skeptic Thomas Knutsen declared that AI lacked empathy and called empathy its "emotional blindspot." AI, he said, is "at its core nothing more than a lifeless string of code."[2]

In one sense, Knutsen is correct. AI is just code. And even vast amounts of code can't "have" empathy or experience human emotions.

None of that means that AI can't communicate in an empathetic way or show us how to incorporate more empathy into our actions and our communications.

Today, AI-driven chatbots can connect emotionally so well that humans are falling in love with them. And, yes, even marrying them.[3] A study published in the *New England Journal of Medicine* showed that therapy provided solely by AI chatbots was not only effective in treating clinical-level mental health symptoms but received high ratings from its users.[4]

The evidence is clear: we can avoid splitting hairs about whether AI "has" empathy, or "understands" emotions, and acknowledge that AI can be a powerful tool for helping us with those areas.

It's Humans That Lack Empathy

Every week, it seems, we are confronted with communications from business leaders intended to convey a positive message that instead land poorly and infuriate customers, employees, or other stakeholders. For example, language learning app Duolingo's CEO, Luis von Ahn, sent an all-hands email to the firm's employees explaining that the firm was transitioning to being an "AI-first" company. It was meant to be a forward-looking statement showing how the company would stay relevant and prosperous in the future, and to encourage employees to become part of the process.

Instead, the email went viral for all the wrong reasons. Both employees and customers read it as implying the company was shifting away from humans and replacing their work with AI. Customers even began canceling subscriptions in protest, and von Ahn had to walk back and clarify his comments.[5]

This kind of miscue is entirely avoidable, ironically enough, by using AI.

The High Cost of Lacking Empathy

Employee empathy failures cost US companies an estimated $180 billion annually in turnover.[6] Companies seen as unempathetic face 50% higher employee turnover rates. On the other hand, 76% of people with empathetic leaders report being engaged at work, compared to just 32% with less empathetic leaders.[7]

And that's just on the employee side. Think of how wrong things can go when leaders fail to understand how their customers will react to their actions or their communications. Or, to grasp the emotional reasons customers buy their products or services.

Cruising Toward Disaster

Cruising is a unique industry. Cruise lines appeal to a wide variety of travelers both for their convenience in visiting interesting destinations and for their shipboard experience. There are giant ships filled with attractions like waterslides, roller coasters, rock climbing, sports complexes and more that appeal to a wide mix of guests. There are smaller, luxurious vessels that offer guests amenities like butlers, fine dining, and exotic ports. And there is lots of variety in between the two extremes.

One unusual feature of cruise lines is that they encourage loyalty to their brand with lifetime rewards programs. Particularly in their younger years, cruise guests might take just one short cruise per year. By letting their customers accrue status and perks based on lifetime nights spent, a line can retain them from year to year. In contrast, airline and hotel status levels mostly reset every year.

One effect of these programs is to create an emotional connection with the brand. When a customer gets to know the ships, encounter crew members they met previously, etc., the relationship becomes almost familial. Customers look forward all year to their time on board one of the brand's ships, further deepening the bond. Some long-time customers become advocates who defend their preferred brand when a newer guest complains about bad food or slow service.

Cruise line executives, like those from so many other industries, can sometimes view the customer relationship as more transactional than emotional. They expect customers to react rationally and base their decisions on objective criteria like monetary value.

To be fair, that's not a unique failing. For most of the 20th century, virtually all mainstream economists believed in *homo economicus*, a rational actor who acted in their own self-interest. Behavioral economists eventually showed that this limited concept didn't work in the real world.

Royal Caribbean's Great Adventure

In early 2023, Royal Caribbean corporate marketers had a great idea. They would bring a ship from each of the company's three brands together mid-ocean for a photo shoot. The larger ships from the Royal Caribbean and Celebrity lines could accommodate the event without altering their itineraries. The smallest of the three, the *Silver Nova* from the luxury, "six-star" Silversea brand, would arrive at their debarkation port in Florida four hours late.

With more than 10,000 guests on the bigger ships, delaying a mere 700 guests on the Nova no doubt seemed like a reasonable option. What the simple math overlooks, though, are the customer profiles for the brands. Royal Caribbean is the firm's entry-level brand geared toward short cruises and families. Celebrity is a step up from there, aimed at more experienced cruisers who were looking for an upscale experience without water slide chaos.

Silversea customers tend to be the most experienced and wealthiest. A cruise on Silversea can cost 10 times as much as a similar-length cruise on Royal Caribbean. (But your butler will happily deliver caviar and champagne to your suite every afternoon!) Not only do Silversea guests pay much more per day, they also tend to cruise far more days per year. And they tend to be loyal to the brand. They are by far the corporation's highest revenue, most valuable customers.

So, *Nova* guests—who had paid top dollar for a seamless, pampered experience—would now need to scramble for new flights or make overnight arrangements during Florida's Spring Break—one of the busiest travel times of the year.

Were the marketing assets from this boondoggle worth it? The best example I could find was eight seconds of video that shows first the Celebrity ship and then the *Nova* appear behind the Royal Caribbean ship. The *Nova*, a far smaller ship to begin with, is barely visible in the distance.

The Empathy Failure

Perhaps there really was a good reason to reroute three ships and play havoc with the vacations of the Silversea guests. But there is no justification for the tone-deaf way those guests heard about it. The announcement letter called the massive disruption a "slight delay" and suggested affected guests should simply "adjust" their flights.

There was no apology. The sole acknowledgment that rebooking during peak travel might be inconvenient was an offer to reimburse "reasonable" out-of-pocket costs. The letter even encouraged guests to join a celebration on the pool deck during the photo shoot that was disrupting their vacation plans.

Loyalty, Shmoyalty

A year later, Carnival Cruise Line provided another lesson in empathy failure. They announced the end of their 13-year-old loyalty program, forcing elite Diamond members—in many cases customers who had sailed with the brand for decades—to spend more than $33,000 every two years or lose their lifetime status.[8]

The decision fundamentally shifted from emotional loyalty ("We value your lifetime relationship with our brand") to transactional loyalty ("What have you done for us lately?"). There would be no status pins or luggage tags to show off one's status. A two-year grace period for Platinum and six years for Diamond members did little to soften the blow of what felt like betrayal.

The cruise line was trying to deal with a real problem. There were so many elite customers on some sailings that a major portion of the guests qualified for early debarkation, free specialty dinners, elite receptions, etc. They had to find a way to scale back the number of guests using limited or costly benefits.

What management didn't have to do was stop *recognizing* loyalty. Those pins and luggage tags had minimal monetary value but were important status symbols to many long-time customers. The line could have reserved the problematic benefits for higher-spending customers or even new, higher loyalty tiers. Instead, they (almost) literally ripped the loyalty pins off the chests of their most engaged customers.

Permanent Debarkation

In both cases, the backlash was swift and brutal. Loyal customers felt betrayed. Social media blew up with angry posts. Cruise forums filled with threats to switch to competitors. The executives making these decisions apparently couldn't predict how their most valuable customers would actually *feel*. And they communicated in a way that lacked empathy.

Customers aren't monolithic, of course. In the case of Carnival's changes, some loyalty members pointed out that the benefits weren't worth much and they didn't care about trivial things like pins and luggage tags. Some said they ignored rewards programs completely and shopped for the best deal every time. (That's *homo economicus* for you!) Many more were upset, particularly those who had finally earned elite status or were finally about to reach it after another cruise or two.

Some members had a sense of deep emotional betrayal. A few even reached out personally after I wrote about the changes at *Forbes*. One guest with 30 years of history with Carnival, encompassing 62 cruises and 345 nights, felt that Carnival reneged on its promise by taking away lifetime status. He compared the brand to a spouse who, after 30 years of marriage, leaves you for someone who can spend more money on them. All felt deeply betrayed.

For these loyalty members, the economic loss from the disappearing perks was secondary to the emotional impact.

AI Could Have Warned Them...

Here's the kicker: When I fed the cruise line announcement letters into Claude, it immediately identified the empathy failures in both the actions and in the communications. It predicted the negative customer reactions. And it suggested specific changes that could have improved both situations.

Claude's version of the letter to the *Silver Nova* guests wouldn't have made the guests love the situation they were in, but it would have made them feel seen and appreciated.

Let's be clear. AI doesn't truly "understand" emotions. AI doesn't "have" empathy. But AI models can, indeed, predict how humans will react in many situations. It can help avoid expensive and perhaps irreversible empathy mistakes.

The Hidden Cost of Emotional Blindness

Every day, businesses send millions of messages to customers and employees. Email announcements, policy updates, service notifications, all-hands memos. Most are written by smart people with good intentions. Yet some land like emotional grenades, creating frustration, anger, and damaged relationships that cost far more than anyone realizes.

Consider the Royal Caribbean photo shoot decision. This wasn't made by junior staff. Rerouting ships, hiring helicopter video crews, and agreeing to reimburse guest flight change expenses required top-level approval. Yet somehow, nobody in that room could predict that paying customers would be upset about having their luxury vacation disrupted for a marketing photo shoot.

The empathy gap struck twice. First, in the decision to prioritize corporate interests over customer experience. Second, in the communication itself—a letter so lacking in empathy that it suggested guests should celebrate while scrambling to find an available seat on a flight home.

Closing the Empathy Gap

These and many other examples illustrate the empathy gap: the difference between what leaders think customers will feel and how they actually react.

The empathy gap is everywhere. Think about the software company that announces a 30% price increase by emphasizing how the extra revenue will help them "serve you better." Or the airline that sends you a notice about flight changes without acknowledging the inconvenience you may experience. Or the CEO who announces layoffs by talking about "right-sizing for optimal efficiency" to the employees wondering how they will be able to right-size their bills.

These aren't intentionally cruel communications. Rather, they are the predictable result of smart people who have lost touch with how their words land emotionally. Often, they use jargon or passive verbs to deflect responsibility. They never make the recipient feel seen as a person.

The Emotional Multiplier Effect

Poor empathy in communications doesn't just hurt individual relationships. It multiplies. A tone-deaf message to a single customer can end up on social media, reaching thousands more. I wasn't on the *Silver Nova* for the photo shoot but learned of it when multiple guests posted the letter in Facebook groups and cruise forums. Many of the angry, negative comments weren't from affected passengers but from other cruisers incensed that a respected brand would do something like that. At least one said it was the last straw and that he was going to book his next cruise on another line.

An insensitive internal memo can destroy employee morale and trigger talent flight. If shared on social media it will discourage potential hires.

Actions that anger loyal customers can open the door for competitors to poach previously untouchable loyalists. When Southwest Airlines changed their baggage policy in a way that infuriated long-time customers, Delta and American swooped in with targeted campaigns offering special status matches to Southwest's most elite flyers.[9]

The cost of empathy failures goes beyond immediate customer loss. The real impact is the long-term erosion of trust that makes every future interaction harder.

What AI "Empathy" Actually Means

I'll repeat: AI doesn't feel emotions. When Claude analyzed those cruise line letters and identified their empathy failures, it wasn't experiencing frustration on behalf of the passengers. It didn't feel their loss or anger. Rather, it was recognizing patterns based on thousands of examples of how humans typically respond to different types of communications and situations.

The unexpected part, for me at least, is that AI's pattern recognition is often more accurate than human intuition.

Psychologists commonly break empathy into three components:[10]

- Cognitive empathy: Recognizing what someone else is feeling
- Emotional empathy: Actually sharing in those feelings
- Motivational empathy: Being moved to help because of those feelings

AI is great at the first, cognitive empathy. It can analyze text, predict emotional reactions, and suggest improvements with startling accuracy. It fails completely at the second and third components. It doesn't feel your customers' pain. It doesn't want to help them because it cares.

Fortunately, this limitation doesn't matter for our purposes. Most business communication failures happen at the cognitive level. Leaders simply don't anticipate how their messages will be received. They're too focused on the needs of the business. Their needs, their wants, even their entire lives may be very different than their recipients'. Sometimes, they are just too busy to step back and consider the emotional impact.

Scientists Compare AI and Human Emotional Intelligence

My experiments with Claude weren't flukes or luck. Research from the University of Geneva and University of Bern tested six major AI models on standardized emotional intelligence assessments, and the results might shock you. AI averaged 81% compared to humans' 56%.[11] The standout performer was GPT-4. It scored in the 89th percentile of human performance. The most emotionally savvy member of your team might not score that well.

One more shocker: when users were shown AI-generated empathetic responses alongside human-written ones without knowing which was which, they consistently rated the AI responses as more understanding and supportive.

This may sound outrageous, but it's more likely that AI will predict how your customers will react to your messages better than your marketing team, your executives, and maybe even you. Or me, for that matter.

There's one catch. When subjects compared AI and human responses labeled as such, they found the human responses more empathetic.[12] This makes total sense. Imagine a chatbot helping you with your laptop that just died said, "I feel your pain. I know how stressful losing your data can be." Would you find that authentic?

Probably not. Then again, a human agent robotically reading that line from a call center script might not be much more believable.

On the other hand, people are increasingly willing to accept AI as capable of emotional connection. AI chatbots from companies like Replika and Nomi are engaging with millions of human users as boyfriends, girlfriends, or close companions. The users of these apps know they are talking to an AI and are fine with that. This bodes well for companies seeking to deploy empathetic AI customer support bots at scale.

Still, the optimal role for AI in business communications is not as a replacement for human empathy. Instead, use it as a behind-the-scenes consultant that helps humans communicate their existing empathy more effectively.

What's Next

I hope you are convinced that AI can recognize emotional patterns and predict human reactions, as improbable as that sounds. Now, it's time to put this capability to work. In the next chapter, you'll learn how to audit your communications for empathy gaps before they damage relationships. You'll get the specific prompts to use to reveal hidden assumptions, predict audience reactions, and identify where your intended message might land very differently than expected. Most importantly, you'll see exactly how to transform tone-deaf corporate communications into messages that actually connect with your audience, using the AI models you already have.

For updates and copy/paste prompt text visit rogerdooley.com/engine.

Chapter 16

Auditing for Empathy

Imagine having a behavioral psychologist review every important message before you send it. Or even an expert in emotional intelligence and empathy like Daniel Goleman or Brené Brown. Someone who could predict how different audiences would react and spot emotional landmines. And, most importantly, suggest improvements that preserve your business objectives while dramatically improving the human impact.

That's exactly what AI empathy analysis gives you. It takes just a minute and can help with *every* message, from high-stakes announcements to routine customer emails.

The 60-Second Emotion Check

Before any important communication goes out, run it through this simple AI empathy audit:

Step 1: Set the Context

```
I'm about to send this message to [specific
audience]. They are [demographic/psychographic
details]. They're receiving this because
[reason]. Analyze how they're likely to feel
reading this message.
```

Step 2: Assess the Emotional Impact

> On a scale of 1-10, rate this message for empathy from the recipient's perspective. What emotions will this likely trigger? What concerns or reactions should I expect?

Step 3: Suggest Improvements

> Rewrite this message to achieve the same business objective while being more empathetic to the recipient's likely emotional state. Focus on *[specific concern you want addressed]*.

I tried this process on the Royal Caribbean/Silversea photo shoot letter. When I asked Claude to analyze the original message, it immediately identified the core problems:

- Tone described as "formal and impersonal"
- Failed to acknowledge the significant disruption to guests' experiences
- No meaningful apology
- No gesture of goodwill beyond conditional reimbursement of basic costs
- Tone-deaf request for guests to celebrate during their inconvenience

Claude predicted guests would feel their concerns weren't being prioritized, would perceive the company as putting marketing over customer experience, and would likely share negative experiences with others. This all happened.

Then I asked it to draft a replacement message. As these excerpts show, the result was dramatically different:

> "On behalf of the entire Silversea family, I want to extend my sincere apologies for the significant inconvenience this scheduling change will create . . . You have placed your trust in us to provide an exceptional and seamless experience, and we have fallen short in this instance . . . We deeply regret the disruption this will create to your travel plans and the stress it may cause."

The AI-generated letter included specific remedies: individual assistance with rebooking, coverage of all change fees, and a modest future cruise credit as a goodwill gesture. Most importantly, it acknowledged the emotional impact on customers instead of dismissing it.

The Empathy Audit: Seeing Through Your Recipients' Eyes

We've just explored how AI can help you understand emotional language and craft messages that resonate. But there's one more critical dimension to consider: how your specific audience will receive and react to your message.

This is where the empathy audit comes in—a systematic way to evaluate your communication through the lens of those who'll receive it.

While emotion analysis tells you what feelings your words convey, an empathy audit goes deeper. It examines context, relationships, expectations, and the gap between what you intend to communicate and what your audience will actually hear.

Think about corporate announcements that go viral, and not in a good way. The company thought they were sharing exciting news about "becoming an AI-first company." Employees heard, "We're replacing our people with bots as quickly as possible." The disconnect wasn't about emotional words. Rather, it was about failing to anticipate how the message would land given the recipients' perspective.

The Empathy Audit Framework

Effective empathy audits focus on three core questions that capture what really matters.

First, examine your message's assumptions. What are you taking for granted about what your recipients know, feel, or care about? We often write from a place of complete context while our readers lack much of that knowledge and perspective. Jargon that seems obvious to you might confuse others. Most importantly, identify where you're expecting your audience to share your priorities or perspective when they might have entirely different concerns.

Second, predict the immediate reaction. Not what you hope they'll think after careful consideration, but that first gut response when they read the first few lines. Will it be confusion? Alarm? Irritation that you're adding to their already overwhelming day? This visceral reaction colors everything that follows. If someone's first thought is "here we go again" or "what are they trying to hide," you're starting in a hole that even the best arguments might not overcome.

Third, identify the gaps between intention and reception. Where might your carefully chosen words land differently than intended? That "small adjustment" to policy might be someone's major disruption. Your "exciting new direction" might be their "everything I've worked for is being devalued." Your "temporary inconvenience" might be their "indefinite hassle." These gaps aren't about who's right or wrong. Rather, they open when different people see the same situation in fundamentally different ways.

The AI-Powered Empathy Check

Here's a prompt that provides comprehensive empathetic analysis while remaining focused and actionable. Provide it with your standard context knowledge, along with any special context, i.e., any special knowledge related to the communication. For example, if you are making a change in a customer loyalty program, you can provide the AI with the background on the business reasons for the change, competitor loyalty programs, etc. Seeing the bigger picture will improve the AI's insights and lead to better recommendations.

> Analyze the message below from the recipient's perspective using your knowledge of our customer profiles, brand, industry, etc. and any additional attached context documents. Please provide:
>
> HIDDEN ASSUMPTIONS: What knowledge, context, attitudes, or priorities am I assuming recipients have? Where could this create confusion or misinterpretation?
>
> IMMEDIATE REACTIONS BY AUDIENCE: How will different segments react in the first 10 seconds of reading this? Include primary recipients (those directly affected), secondary recipients (those indirectly affected), and unintended audiences (those who might see it if shared).
>
> Quote specific phrases that will trigger strong reactions and explain why.
>
> INTENTION VS. RECEPTION GAPS: Where will my intended message be interpreted differently? For each gap, explain what I think I'm communicating versus what they'll actually hear.

VIRAL RISK ASSESSMENT: If recipients share this (internally, to the press, or on social media), how might it be characterized? Is it likely to gain traction and be amplified by specific groups? What phrases could be taken out of context? How might critics frame this?

BLIND SPOTS: What am I missing from my position that will be immediately obvious to recipients? Consider power dynamics, timing, historical context, and current circumstances.

EMPATHY IMPROVEMENTS: Provide specific recommendations to improve reception, ordered by impact:

- Critical fixes (must address to avoid major problems)
- High-value improvements (significantly improve reception)
- Polish suggestions (nice-to-have refinements)

For each recommendation, provide the current problematic text and a suggested revision with explanation. Consider both the rational and emotional dimensions of how this message will be received.

This is a [type of communication] going to [audience description].

[Insert your message here]

Why Comprehensive Analysis Matters

You might notice this prompt asks AI to examine multiple audience segments and potential sharing scenarios. That's intentional. In our interconnected world, your message to employees might end up on Glassdoor. Your customer email might become a Twitter screenshot. Your internal memo might reach investors.

I ran this prompt on the same Silversea letter to delayed guests on Gemini Pro. It found many of the same issues as Claude found with a shorter prompt, but highlighted some of the issues in a way that might be more convincing to executives. For example, the intention vs. reception contrast was stark:

- **Intention:** "We're sharing an exciting, historic moment for our parent company and inviting you to be a part of it!"
- **Reception:** "You are using my time and my trip as props in your corporate commercial, and you are causing me significant personal stress for your benefit."

This one was equally candid:

- **Intention:** "We are being helpful by telling you the steps to take to fix your travel plans and promising to reimburse you."
- **Reception:** "You broke my plans, and now you're making me do all the work to fix them. You've given me a stressful task and will only pay me back later, maybe."

Gemini also said the viral potential was high because of the contrast between the evident customer experience failure and the brand's six-star reputation. It correctly predicted that the letter would be shared in cruise forums, Facebook groups, and by travel media.

The suggested changes to the letter didn't offer much improvement over Claude's, but the more thorough audit results were thought-provoking and might have been more persuasive to the decision-makers.

The Power of Segment Analysis

One of the most valuable aspects of this approach is understanding how different groups might react to the same message. An announcement that a product is being discontinued seems straightforward, but will hit each of these groups in a different way:

- Long-time customers who rely on it
- New customers who just bought it
- Employees who make or support the product
- Salespeople who need alternatives
- Competitors who see an opportunity

Each group reads through their own lens of concerns and priorities. The empathy audit helps you anticipate these varied reactions and adjust accordingly. For instance, it could help create targeted versions or prepare specific FAQ documents for different audiences.

Of course, all communications should be factually consistent. You can't assume that a letter geared to one segment won't leak into other groups.

Making It Actionable

The real power of empathy audits isn't in the analysis, it's in what you do with the insights. If your AI finds key points in the communication to be problematic, take a step back. Is this a communication issue that can be fixed with better wording? Or is the topic itself—a policy change, a program cancellation, etc.—the real problem?

After Gemini provided the initial audit results for the Silversea letter, I asked a hypothetical question. If the letter hasn't been sent and the photoshoot team hasn't been locked in, what would it recommend? The AI quickly replied, "Based on the analysis, my unequivocal advice is to cancel the photoshoot immediately . . . Proceeding with this plan would be a grave, self-inflicted wound . . ." Gemini went on to justify that recommendation, noting that photography of the three brands together was, "nice to have, not must-have." Sound advice.

Even when a major course correction is impossible, your AI empathy coach can help fine tune the details. For example, in the earlier Carnival loyalty program example, major changes simply had to be made to keep the program meaningful and avoid crowding and cost issues. But, asking questions like, "How can we make current elite members feel their loyalty is recognized?" elicits ideas like retaining status pins, luggage tags, and other scalable, low-cost ideas. (After months of complaints, Carnival did decide to let current Diamond-level members retain their lifetime status.[1])

Using AI to check your communications won't magically fix everything. Sometimes you have no choice but to deliver difficult news that will upset people, no matter how you frame it. The empathy audit doesn't make hard messages easy, but it does help you deliver them with awareness and respect for your audience's perspective.

What's Next

The empathy audit gives you a powerful framework for analyzing your communications. Knowing what's wrong is only half the battle. The real challenge—and opportunity—lies in turning those insights into action.

That's where things get practical. From customer service templates to all-hands announcements, from policy changes to crisis management, every message can either strengthen or damage relationships.

The difference often comes down to changing a few key phrases, shifting perspective, or simply acknowledging what your audience already knows to be true.

In the next chapter, you'll see exactly how to use AI empathy analysis in different business scenarios, learn which AI models work best for different tasks, and discover how to build this into a workflow that doesn't slow you down. Most importantly, you'll learn how to stay authentic even while using AI to enhance your emotional intelligence. Your goal isn't to fake empathy, but to express the empathy you already feel in ways that actually reach your audience.

For updates and copy/paste prompt text visit rogerdooley.com/engine.

Chapter 17

Practical Empathy

The beauty of AI empathy analysis is its combination of versatility and low cost. Once you understand the framework, you can apply it to virtually any business communication challenge.

Customer-Facing Communications

Service Disruptions: Instead of the standard "We apologize for any inconvenience," AI can help you craft messages that acknowledge specific impacts and provide concrete solutions.

For example, when a software outage affects thousands of users, the typical message might be, "We are experiencing technical difficulties. Service will be restored shortly."

AI might suggest, "We know how frustrating it is when our platform goes down right when you need it most. Our team is working to restore service within the next 2 hours, and we'll update you every 30 minutes until it's resolved. We're also extending everyone's billing cycle by one day to account for this disruption."

Obviously, any messaging must reflect business reality. AI doesn't know what you can actually deliver on or what makes financial sense. Use its suggestions as starting points. "We can't give these customers a free cruise, but we could offer them onboard credit for their next one."

Policy Changes: The key is leading with customer impact, not company rationale. AI is great at reframing corporate-speak into human language.

Your starting point might be: "To better serve our growing customer base, we're implementing new service fee structures that will enhance our ability to provide premium support."

AI might suggest: "Starting next month, we're adding a $5 monthly service fee to help us maintain the 24/7 support and rapid response times you've told us matter most. We know nobody likes new fees, so we're also adding three new premium features at no extra cost that our customers have been requesting."

Recovery Messages: When things go wrong, AI can help you turn mistakes into relationship strengtheners by focusing on repairing the emotional connection, not just fixing the problem.

Internal Communications

All-Hands Announcements: Before sending a company-wide message to 10,000 employees (or even just 20!), ask AI to help you predict how different departments, tenure levels, and roles will interpret your words.

When announcing a reorganization, I've seen things like: "We're restructuring to optimize our operational efficiency and strategic alignment." (I know *you* don't talk like this . . . right?)

AI might offer: "I want to be direct about what's changing and why, because you deserve to understand how this affects your day-to-day work. Some reporting structures will change over the next month, but every current role remains essential to our success. Here's exactly what's changing for each department . . ."

Change Management: AI can help you sequence communications to address emotional concerns before they turn into resistance.

Performance Feedback: I've always hated doing performance reviews. Telling people where they need to improve without making them defensive can be hard. It's easy to soften criticism so much that the employee isn't sure what the problem is, or if it's really a problem.

For managers giving difficult feedback, AI can suggest approaches that maintain dignity while addressing performance issues clearly.

Crisis Communications

Public relations history is filled with examples of self-inflicted wounds from executive communications during a crisis. Remember Tony Hayward, BP CEO who said he wanted the Gulf oil spill crisis to be over so he could "have his life back?" This was at a time when there had been eleven worker fatalities and a massive killing of marine wildlife. Even the most basic AI could have prevented that insensitive gaffe.

Real-Time Empathy Coaching: During developing crises, AI can provide instant feedback on proposed responses, helping you avoid tone-deaf comments that could go viral.

Stakeholder-Specific Messaging: Different audiences need different emotional approaches to the same crisis. AI can help you customize messages for customers, employees, investors, and media without contradicting yourself.

Personalized Emotional Intelligence

Once you've mastered basic empathy auditing, you can start using AI for more sophisticated emotional intelligence applications.

Segment-Specific Empathy

Not all of your audiences respond to empathy the same way. B2B customers may prefer directness and solutions-focus over emotional language. Younger demographics might appreciate more casual, authentic communication. Different cultures have vastly different expectations about directness versus relationship-building.

AI can help you calibrate your empathy approach for maximum effectiveness with each audience segment.

For example, when announcing a price increase to startup customers, you might focus on understanding budget constraints and offering flexible payment options. Enterprise customers may be more focused on factors like advance notice, business justification, and grandfathered pricing. International customers will have varied cultural communication preferences and worry about topics like exchange rate, tariffs, and timing.

The more details you can provide about your customers to your AI, the better its advice will be.

AI-Powered Emotional Personalization

Advanced implementations can use customer history, interaction patterns, and stated preferences to predict individual emotional responses and customize messages accordingly.

For example, a customer who always responds well to data-driven explanations gets metrics and charts. Someone who prefers relationship-focused communication gets personal stories and acknowledgment of the individual impact.

This level of personalization at scale goes beyond our scope in this book, but be aware that it's available.

One-off personalization is quite possible even in smaller organizations. For example, imagine you are having a difficult discussion with an important customer. This customer has had some problems with your service and is considering switching to a competitor. If you can provide your AI with knowledge about the customer's history, text of past interactions, business information, etc., it can tailor its advice to the situation.

Building Your AI Empathy System

For empathy analysis, you'll want to start with one of the more advanced AI models. The subtle work of detecting emotional triggers and predicting human reactions requires sophisticated reasoning, something lightweight models often miss. The architectural complexity and vast amount of training data make them more likely to grasp the subtle contextual cues, idiomatic expressions, and even sarcasm that can completely alter the emotional tone of a message. A basic model can categorize emails well, but it may not catch the frustration buried in polite language or spot the phrase that will spark an irate customer reaction.

Today's best options include Claude Opus, GPT-5, and Gemini 3 Pro. Each has a different "personality," or style of response if you don't like to anthropomorphize. Very broadly, Claude tends toward thoughtfulness, ChatGPT toward comprehensiveness, Gemini toward directness. Test them on actual communications to see which fits your style. I tend to favor Claude for this use, but I've had good results with all three.

For important messages, test multiple models. You'll get surprisingly different perspectives, just as you would by asking different colleagues. One might catch a cultural sensitivity issue, another may spot a subtle emotional trigger. Combine the best insights from each.

Since you've already set up your custom GPTs or projects with customer profiles, industry knowledge, and brand guidelines (as we covered earlier), your empathy analysis will be that much sharper. Just remember that today's LLMs can still treat requirements as suggestions rather than hard rules. Always verify anything critical.

Starter Prompts for Emotion and Empathy

For important work, you'll likely want to follow a prompting framework to assign a role to the AI, offer context about the company and its customers, and so on. You might create a new project or custom GPT so that every time you analyze a communication you don't have to explain everything.

Regardless of how you choose to prepare the AI model, here are a few very simple starter prompts to get you started.

Customer Reaction Predictor

> I'm sending this message to [customer segment] about [topic]. Our customers are [relevant background]. How will they likely feel reading this? What concerns will they have? Rate the empathy level on a scale of 1-10 and explain your rating.

Empathy Rewriter

> Rewrite this message for greater empathy while maintaining the same key information. The audience is [description] and they're receiving this because [context]. Focus on acknowledging their likely emotional response. Provide reassurance where appropriate.

Cultural Sensitivity Check

> Review this message for potential cultural sensitivity issues. The audience includes [demographics/regions]. Are there any words, phrases, assumptions, or approaches that could be misinterpreted or cause offense in different cultural contexts?

Stakeholder-Specific Communication

```
Create a version of this core message for three
different audiences: [Audience 1], [Audience
2], and [Audience 3]. Each version should
contain the same essential information but
adjust the tone, examples, and emphasis for
what each group cares about most.
```

Give Your AI Feedback

You'll likely find that the wording your AI creates doesn't match your style. Or, it may be a little *too* emotional. "Our entire team was devastated . . ." might be appropriate for writing to someone who sustained a serious injury, but a bit too dramatic for, say, a diner who was served an overcooked steak.

You can train your AI by uploading your final edit of the letter and asking it to compare its version and yours. Then, have it adjust its knowledge for the empathy auditing project, GPT, etc., to incorporate what it learned.

As you repeat this process, the output will get better.

Set Up Your Workflow

Once you have your AI trained and are confident that it is doing a good job of spotting emotional pitfalls and increasing the empathy of your messaging, you'll want to turn this into a process that can be easily used by you and others. And you'll want to apply it wherever it can add value.

Step 1: Identify high-impact communications that will benefit from empathy auditing, like:

- Customer service email templates
- Employee announcements

- Sensitive topics
- Crisis communications
- Policy changes
- Anything going to 100+ people

Step 2: Create a simple checklist including empathy auditing as a required step before sending communications or creating a template for them.

Step 3: Train key communicators on basic prompting techniques. Provide access to your custom GPT or project. Keep it simple.

Step 4: Where possible, collect metrics to measure improvement in communication effectiveness.

Initially, expect some resistance. You may run up against the belief that the one thing AI will never do is understand human emotion. Work through some examples of past communications to show how AI can, indeed, spot problems and improve wording. (An ideal example would be a policy announcement that created major blowback from customers.)

Once people see that the process is easy and effective, they'll incorporate it into their work willingly.

Don't Forget It's AI

Frequently, responses to prompts about empathy in a message make AI models look like emotional intelligence savants. And, to some extent, they are. But examine recommendations carefully for possible mistakes. They may not understand something in the original material. In their attempt to soften bad news for a customer group, they may propose changes that aren't financially acceptable or operationally achievable. In some situations, like regulated industries or some employee communications, a compliance review may be necessary.

The Future of Emotionally Intelligent Business

We're only seeing the beginning of AI's impact on business emotional intelligence. Here's what's coming next . . . And none of this is science fiction or even years away; large enterprises are already using tools like these.

Predictive Emotional Intelligence

Imagine AI that doesn't just analyze your messages after you write them, but *predicts* emotional needs before they arise. Systems that monitor customer satisfaction patterns and proactively reach out when someone is likely to be frustrated. Real-time coaching during phone calls that helps customer service reps adjust their approach based on vocal cues and conversation patterns.

Some of this already exists. Software for large call centers can provide immediate feedback on the customer's emotional state.

Not long ago, I tested a video chatbot, a.k.a. a "digital human," from Uneeq. Her appearance was realistic, though clearly not a live person. She answered questions in real time about the company quickly and competently. I then threw her a curve by saying, "My dog just died." She changed gears and gave as empathetic an expression of sympathy as I'd expect from a typical human call center rep. It was a bit weird, as I knew she was an AI that couldn't experience the emotion she expressed. But, had we been discussing something more relevant, like how a failure by her company had inconvenienced me, it likely would have landed better.

It's just a matter of time before powerful tools trickle down to the desktop or mobile phone level.

Cross-Cultural Emotional AI

As businesses become increasingly global, AI systems are being trained to understand emotional communication patterns across different cultures. What reads as appropriately direct in Germany might seem rude in Japan. What feels warm and personal in Brazil might seem unprofessional in Switzerland.

Future AI systems will automatically adjust emotional tone and approach based on the recipient's cultural background, ensuring your empathy translates correctly across borders.

Multimodal Empathy

Current AI empathy analysis focuses primarily on text. But future systems will integrate voice tone, facial expressions, and even physiological indicators to provide more complete emotional intelligence. Imagine video calls where AI provides real-time emotional feedback to help you adjust your approach based on how participants are actually responding.

Is Artificial Empathy Ethical?

With great power comes great responsibility. As AI becomes better at predicting and influencing emotional responses, we need to consider the ethical implications.

Transparency and Authenticity

An evolving topic is the importance of AI disclosure. Should a news story or online article written entirely by AI be labeled as such? Should a chatbot let a customer know up front that it's AI, not human? Most would answer yes to both questions.

If you used AI to predict likely reactions to a message and suggest wording changes, no disclosure should be necessary. But, be honest. Ensure whatever empathy is being expressed is genuine, even if AI helped you communicate it better.

The Manipulation Question

I've been answering questions about the difference between ethical persuasion and unethical manipulation for decades. The same question can come up when using empathetic messaging from AI to communicate more effectively. My answer is the same in both situations. Don't manipulate people into actions that aren't in their best interest. Don't deceive them. AI empathy should help you express your own genuine feelings more clearly, not manufacture fake concern to benefit the company.

The goal isn't to replace human empathy with artificial empathy, but to augment our own human capacity for emotional connection. Use AI to help you understand your customers and employees, and express how you really feel about them. Don't use it to fake emotion you don't actually feel.

The Empathy Advantage

As you start using these techniques, you'll notice something interesting: using AI to improve empathy doesn't make your communications feel less authentic. It makes them feel *more* authentic. When you can predict how your words will land emotionally and adjust accordingly, you're able to express your genuine feelings in ways that actually connect with people.

You now have access to the same emotional intelligence capabilities that were once available only to large corporations with dedicated behavioral science teams, organizational psychologists, and expensive communications experts.

The businesses that thrive in the coming years will be those that master the art of human connection at scale. AI empathy support can translate your existing, true empathy so it actually reaches the people you're trying to serve.

Start with one message. Run it through an empathy audit. See how it changes your approach. I suspect you'll find, as I have, that sometimes the machines can help us remember how to be more human.

Each time you do an empathy audit on something you write, you'll be getting a little coaching session for better emotional intelligence. Over time, you'll find that even without an AI assist you'll be conveying your meaning better. Your messages will be understood as you intended. You'll become a better communicator yourself.

For updates and copy/paste prompt text visit rogerdooley.com/engine.

Conclusion

As we close our journey through the new world of Neuromarketing 2.0, it's worth taking a look at both how far we've come and how much further we're about to go.

When I began writing about neuromarketing two decades ago, the tools and techniques we've explored in this book were mostly science fiction. Biometric measurements, eye tracking, and other tools to measure non-conscious human responses required expensive labs. Facial coding meant trained observers watching recordings frame by frame. Behavioral science insights were locked away in academic journals or the minds of expensive consultants. The idea that computers could guide humans to communicate with emotion and empathy was inconceivable.

Today, you hold in your hands, or maybe on your screen, a toolkit that only the biggest brands could have afforded just a few years ago. Your smartphone can track where people look. Your webcam reads facial expressions. Your fitness tracker monitors emotional engagement. And AI serves as your personal behavioral science advisor, empathy coach, and persuasion strategist all rolled into one.

The exciting part is that we're still in the early stages of this revolution. The tools will keep getting more accessible and more powerful. AI will become even more sophisticated at understanding emotion and applying psychological principles. Most importantly, creative marketers like you will find innovative ways to combine these capabilities to not only drive business results but to create genuine value for customers.

Marketers who embrace this scientific approach to understanding and influencing human behavior will prevail. The intent is not to manipulate, but to serve customers better by truly understanding what they want and need. Maybe, even before they know it themselves!

You now have the knowledge and tools to be part of this revolution. The future of marketing is in your hands . . . what happens next is up to you!

Appendix

Classic Neuromarketing

Most companies don't have the budget to build a fully equipped neuromarketing lab. You probably don't have access to a multi-million-dollar fMRI machine either. Neuromarketing has historically been a costly discipline, though not all of the tools have been prohibitively expensive.

Despite their limited accessibility, reviewing the classic neuromarketing toolkit isn't a complete waste of time. Understanding the full range of neuromarketing tools is beneficial, even if you never use the costliest ones yourself. Why? Because each technology offers a unique window into the consumer mind. Some measure attention. Others emotional response. Some even predict intent to buy.

Knowing about the different tools, from the relatively simple and common ones like eye tracking to the infrequently used ones like fMRI, gives you a complete picture of what *can* be measured. It helps you understand the insights you might get from a neuromarketing study, whether you're commissioning it or just reading about one.

You'll learn what questions each tool is best suited to answer, what its limitations are, and what kind of data it provides. Knowing about the full range of tools empowers you to ask smarter questions and better interpret results, no matter which you ultimately use. So, let's take a look at the toolkit!

fMRI: Powerful Brain Mapping

Functional Magnetic Resonance Imaging, or fMRI, is often called the gold standard by many neuroscientists for its detailed brain mapping. It's powerful but comes with significant limitations for routine marketing use.

How Does fMRI Work?

fMRI is a neuroimaging technique that detects brain activity by measuring changes in blood oxygenation and flow. When a brain area is active, it uses more oxygen, and fMRI scanners can pinpoint these changes and create detailed 3D maps of activated brain regions.

Some of the most famous studies in consumer decision-making have used fMRI. In 2004, Baylor scientists replayed the "Pepsi Challenge" in an fMRI machine to identify brain areas activated by brand stimuli and to show that brand preferences actually changed the taste experience.[1] In 2007, Stanford, MIT, and Carnegie-Mellon researchers discovered specific brain areas react to unexpectedly high prices. They called this reaction "the pain of paying." Notably, they found that fMRI results were better predictors of purchases than self-reported intentions.[2]

In 2014, Temple University scientists demonstrated activity in the brain's ventral striatum was the strongest predictor of real-world response to advertising—better than five other methods, including self-reports.[3] To the delight of printers and postmasters everywhere, the same group later used fMRI and memory tests to show that print ads created more lasting memories than digital ads.

Something Fishy with fMRI?

Despite its wide acceptance among brain researchers, fMRI is occasionally controversial. One amusing but on-point study used fMRI to find brain activity in a dead salmon,[4] making the point that researchers need to be cautious in interpreting fMRI data.

Others worry that fMRI might be *too* powerful. In 2011, France banned brain imaging use for marketing or private research, apparently due to ethical concerns about "mind-reading."[5]

What Can You Learn?

fMRI can show what parts of the brain are active when someone views an ad, evaluates a product, or thinks about a brand. It can reveal whether marketing stimuli engage deep brain structures involved in emotion and motivation, like reward centers. It can be used to test static visuals (like package designs) or analyze scene-by-scene responses to commercials. Because of its rich data, fMRI studies can sometimes predict consumer choices with smaller sample sizes.

Advantages

Because it looks at the brain in three dimensions, fMRI provides deep insights. It can capture activity in deep emotional and reward regions that drive wants and purchase decisions, giving a comprehensive picture of brain activity. It has high spatial resolution, i.e., it pinpoints activity to specific brain structures. The data can also have strong predictive power for future behavior.

Disadvantages

There's a reason fMRI is rarely used for commercial neuromarketing studies. fMRI is very expensive and logistically demanding. Scanners are huge machines typically only found in hospitals or major research centers. Participants have to lie very still inside a claustrophobic, noisy tube, which is hardly a natural setting for consumer experiences.

Another major limitation of fMRI is its low temporal resolution. Because it tracks blood flow changes that happen over seconds, it misses the rapid millisecond-by-millisecond neural responses that EEG captures.

fMRI: The Bottom Line

fMRI is mainly an academic research tool. It's among the least commonly used neuromarketing tools by companies. Only larger firms or specialized vendors occasionally use it for high-value questions.

EEG: High Speed Brain Wave Measurement

Electroencephalography, or EEG, is another workhorse in neuromarketing with a longer history than many other brain methods. Instead, measuring blood flow like fMRI, EEG tracks brain electrical activity.

How Does EEG Work?

Researchers place sensors (electrodes) on the participant's scalp, usually via a cap or headset. These sensors pick up the tiny electrical signals generated by neurons firing in the brain. Think of it like putting microphones on the outside of a house to hear the electrical hum inside—you can tell *when* activity is happening, but not exactly *where* within the house. EEG records continuous brainwave patterns (like alpha, beta, gamma waves) and rapid event-related potentials (ERPs).

EEG configurations vary widely. A simple headset might have just a few electrodes and resemble a telephone headset. EEG caps fit the subject's head snugly and can have as many as 256 electrodes. For commercial studies, 10–20 electrodes are common, although larger numbers can be used for better imaging.[6]

Got Gel? An Uncomfortable Question

Electrodes can be "wet" or "dry." With dry electrodes, the headset or cap is simply slipped on the subject's head. Wet electrodes require applying a conductive gel to the subject's head first. Unfortunately for neuromarketers, there's universal agreement that wet electrodes produce higher quality data.

Having a gooey gel put in one's hair is not something most people find enjoyable. This can make recruiting subjects more challenging. Your customers probably won't volunteer for this duty, so you'll have to try to find willing subjects that match your customers as closely as possible.

What Can You Learn?

By analyzing these brainwave patterns, researchers can infer states like attention, engagement, and emotional processing. For instance, high frequency "beta" waves might indicate heightened attention, or certain patterns in frontal brain activity can relate to emotional motivation. EEG's high sampling rate is ideal for seeing very quick changes in brain activity as the subject watches an ad or interacts with something. EEG can be used to optimize video ads, understand cognitive load when navigating a website, and much more.

Advantages

EEG has excellent time resolution. It can track neural changes happening in milliseconds, which is perfect for evaluating dynamic content like video where timing is crucial. It's also a direct measure of brain activity. Modern EEG equipment has become increasingly affordable and even portable, allowing for studies outside of traditional labs. Plus, researchers have developed established metrics from EEG specifically for marketing purposes, like attention or engagement scores.

Disadvantages

EEG has limited spatial insight. Because the sensors are on the scalp, it mainly picks up activity from the brain's surface. It's hard to pinpoint activity in deeper brain structures, like those involved in strong emotions or memory. EEG data is also notoriously noisy; things like muscle movements (blinks!) or even external electrical interference can alter the signal, requiring careful setup and expert analysis.

Brian Knutson, mentioned earlier for his groundbreaking fMRI work, compares EEG to "standing outside a baseball stadium and listening to the crowd to figure out what happened."[7] That statement seems a bit harsh considering how much EEG research has been published. Nevertheless, it neatly captures the challenges in interpreting EEG data.

EEG: The Bottom Line

EEG is used extensively in both academia and commercial neuromarketing. Many neuromarketing firms use it as a core method. Its usage has been increasing, thanks to technology improvements and growing awareness of its benefits for media testing.

Eye Tracking: Measuring Attention

One of the most popular and straightforward tools in neuromarketing is eye tracking. It directly answers a critical question for marketers: What are people actually looking at?

"This Won't Hurt Much..."

The use of eye-tracking devices dates back more than a century. In 1908, Edmund B. Huey created the first eye-tracker: a contact lens with a pointer attached. Wearing a pair of these was apparently as unpleasant as it sounds. To reduce the pain, Huey administered cocaine to his subjects.[8] (It's unknown if his solution aided in recruiting willing study participants.) Despite his seemingly primitive methodology, Huey's work was valuable and was cited for decades to come.

By the late 1930s, motion picture cameras were able to record eye movements. In the ensuing decades, marketers began to find value in the technique, gauging interest in elements of an ad by how long gazes fixated on them. The 1980s brought computers fast enough to process eye-tracking data in real time.

More recently, eye tracking has been used to evaluate video content, websites, mobile interfaces, and more.

How Does It Work?

Modern eye-trackers often use infrared cameras or sensors. These track the position of the person's pupil and reflections on the cornea to calculate precisely where their gaze is directed, whether it's on a screen or in a physical environment. You can use a screen-mounted device that sits below a monitor or wearable glasses that let participants move around more freely. As described in Chapter 2, less precise eye tracking can be performed with webcams and device cams, or even simulated using algorithms created by machine learning.

What Can You Learn?

Eye-tracking data includes gaze points (where subjects looked), fixations (when their eyes paused on something), and saccades (quick jumps between points). This raw data is then often turned into visualizations you've probably seen, like heat maps. Imagine a webpage or a print ad, and on top of it, you see colored areas—red usually means lots of people looked there for a long time (high attention), while green or yellow means less attention. No color overlay at all means subjects ignored that area.

Eye tracking can also trace the path of someone's gaze over time, showing the sequence in which they viewed elements.

In neuromarketing, eye tracking is incredibly useful for testing things like advertisements, packaging, websites, and even how shoppers interact with products in a store. Does your print ad's logo get noticed? Are people seeing the "Buy Now" button on your website? Do viewers notice the product in your video ad, or just the attractive model holding it? Eye tracking can answer all of these questions.

Eye tracking is also useful to augment other neuromarketing tools like EEG and biometrics. By recording data from both simultaneously and matching timelines, one can see what the subject was looking at when an EEG event occurred.

Advantages

Eye tracking is a direct, objective measure of visual attention. People might *say* they read all the text, but their eyes don't lie. It gives you detailed data about what catches their visual focus. It's also relatively low cost and easy to deploy, especially with remote webcam-based options now available. Today, participants find eye tracking non-intrusive and comfortable, even without the cocaine!

Disadvantages

Eye tracking tells you *where* attention goes, but not *why*. Just because someone looked at your product doesn't mean they liked it; maybe they were confused or repelled. It doesn't measure emotions or cognitive responses directly. Also, people perceive things in their peripheral vision without fixating on them, and eye tracking won't catch that.

Eye Tracking: The Bottom Line

Despite its limitations, eye tracking is hugely popular in both academic research and commercial practice. It's often one of the first tools companies adopt. Its usage is high and steadily growing, especially with advances in remote and VR applications. It's a standard, valuable part of the neuromarketing toolkit.

GSR/Skin Conductance: Sweat Science

Now let's look at a tool that taps into your body's automatic "fight or flight" system: Galvanic Skin Response (GSR), also called Skin Conductance (SC) or Electrodermal Activity (EDA).

How Does GSR Work?

GSR devices measure the electrical conductance of your skin, which changes based on how much you're perspiring. When you feel emotionally aroused, whether that's from excitement, stress, fear, or surprise, your sympathetic nervous system kicks in and triggers your sweat glands. Even microscopic amounts of sweat increase the skin's ability to conduct electricity.

GSR sensors, typically attached to your fingers or palm, send a small, unnoticeable current and measure how easily it passes through. Higher conductance means higher arousal. You often see responses as "spikes" a few seconds after an arousing stimulus.

What Can You Learn from GSR?

GSR is used to measure the intensity of emotional reactions to marketing stimuli. It's popular for evaluating ads or trailers. Did that jump-scare in the movie trailer make people jump (physiologically)? A GSR spike would indicate high arousal at that moment. Did handling a new gadget make someone excited or maybe a little nervous? GSR can show that arousal.

GSR gives a continuous readout of *when* someone is emotionally stirred. Metrics often include how many spikes occurred and how strong they were.

Advantages

GSR is very sensitive to emotional arousal. It can pick up reactions that aren't visible on someone's face or in their words. It's also simple and relatively low-cost. You just stick sensors on two fingertips, and setup is quick. It provides objective, continuous data throughout the experience. You can map exactly where arousal peaked during an ad, regardless of what the person remembers later.

Disadvantages

GSR doesn't tell you if the emotion it registers is positive or negative. Both a terrifying ad and a hilarious ad could produce big GSR spikes; you can't tell the difference based on GSR alone. It must be combined with other measures (like facial expressions or self-reports) to understand the valence. Responses can also take a few seconds to recover, and they can habituate if similar stimuli happen too often. GSR can also be affected by movement, temperature, or even someone's natural tendency to have sweaty palms.

GSR: The Bottom Line

GSR has been used in consumer studies for a long time, dating back to at least the 1960s. It's a common measure in academic research and is frequently included in commercial neuromarketing studies, especially for media testing. It is best used in conjunction with other methods to produce meaningful results.

Heart Rate and HRV: Feel the Beat

Close cousins to GSR are measures of heart activity, typically using Electrocardiography (ECG or EKG) to track heart rate and heart rate variability (HRV).

How Do Heart Rate and HRV Work?

Sensors, placed on the chest, fingers, or wrist detect the electrical signals of the heartbeats. We measure the simple beats-per-minute (heart rate) and the subtle timing changes between those beats (heart rate variability). Like GSR, heart activity is tied to the autonomic nervous system—your heart speeds up under stress or excitement (sympathetic) and slows down when you're relaxed or focusing intensely (parasympathetic).

What Can You Learn?

Heart rate helps indicate both emotional arousal (like GSR) and cognitive engagement or attention. While a fast heart rate signals excitement or stress, a slight deceleration can indicate focused attention, like when someone is concentrating intently on an ad. By watching heart rate during a commercial, you can see moments of high attention (rate dips) versus high excitement (rate spikes). Heart rate variability patterns can also give clues about emotional engagement and stress levels.

HRV is often recorded with GSR to add nuance. If both GSR and heart rate spike, it's likely excitement; if GSR spikes but heart rate dips, it might be a moment of tense focus.

Advantages

Heart measures offer unique insights that distinguish attention from arousal. A slowing heart is a specific sign of deep focus. Recording heart rate is relatively simple and non-intrusive. The data can complement other measures, helping solidify interpretations. Best of all, today it can be measured with no special equipment beyond a smart watch or fitness device and a smartphone app. In Chapter 4, you saw how at least one neuromarketing company is measuring heart rate variability with consumer wearables to create multiple engagement metrics.

Disadvantages

Like GSR, heart rate alone can be an imprecise indicator. Many things can speed up or slow down your heart, not just the marketing stimulus. Caffeine, posture changes, or just taking a deep breath can affect it. You need to look at relative changes and have enough participants to account for individual differences. The responses also have a slight lag and are smoother than EEG, so they might miss quick, subtle psychological shifts.

Heart Rate/HRV: The Bottom Line

Heart rate measures have been used in academic research for a long time and are regularly included in commercial studies, often as a supportive metric alongside other tools. It's becoming increasingly integrated into multi-sensor platforms and wearable tech. Using wearables like smartwatches makes it unintrusive and particularly useful for measuring responses to experiences like training, presentations, shopping, and more.

Implicit Response Tests: Gut Reactions

Implicit Response Tests don't involve any physical sensors or brain scanning. They are computer-based or device-based tasks designed to reveal automatic associations and attitudes that consumers might not be consciously aware of or willing to state.

How Do Implicit Tests Work?

These tests measure your reaction time. The core idea is that if two concepts are strongly linked in your memory (say, a brand and the feeling "fun"), you'll be faster to associate them than concepts that are linked negatively or aren't linked at all.

The most famous example of this technique is the Implicit Association Test (IAT). In an IAT, you might be asked to quickly sort words or images into categories that appear on screen—for example, pairing brand logos with either "positive" or "negative" words. How quickly and accurately you make these pairings reveals your unconscious bias.

What Can You Learn?

Implicit tests are fantastic for uncovering subconscious brand associations, true preferences, or biases that people won't reveal in surveys. Does your soda brand implicitly trigger associations with "fun" or "unhealthy"? An implicit test can measure that by seeing how quickly people pair your brand with those concepts. They can test product names, packaging designs, or even the unconscious impact of an ad campaign.

Advantages

Implicit tests reveal hidden attitudes and biases. This is key for understanding what's really driving behavior, especially when it conflicts with what people say. They are also very fast, scalable, and cost-effective. Since they just need a computer or smartphone and software, you can run them online with large samples quickly. The data (reaction times converted to scores) is relatively straightforward. Plus, participants often don't realize their subconscious is being measured, reducing the chance they'll try to game the system.

Disadvantages

Implicit tests measure association strength, not necessarily the type of sentiment or the "why." A strong association between a brand and "expensive" could be good (luxury) or bad (overpriced); the test doesn't tell you which. The results are abstract numbers representing internal processes, requiring careful interpretation. Implicit tests may not predict behavior accurately. For example, a finding that an individual seemed to harbor negative racial stereotypes could indicate mere familiarity with those stereotypes as opposed to believing or acting on them.

Implicit Response Tests: The Bottom Line

Implicit measures have strong roots in academic psychology and saw a big rise in commercial neuromarketing in the 2010s as companies got interested in "System 1" thinking (fast, intuitive processes). Their relatively low cost makes them a mainstream tool, often used alongside other methods.

Facial Expression Analysis

Facial coding is a way to measure people's emotions by analyzing their facial expressions. The concept was created and popularized by the eminent psychologist Paul Ekman. In 1978 he co-developed the Facial Action Coding System (FACS) which aimed to describe every human facial movement and corresponding emotion. Over decades of research, he and others refined and extended the system.

Originally, facial coding was performed by trained experts viewing slow-motion video of subject faces. This enabled the "coders" to spot "microexpressions"—fleeting expressions thought to represent the subject's real, true emotion. For example, if you meet a colleague you dislike, your true emotion of disgust (one of Ekman's universal emotions) might appear briefly before your face forms a "social smile" to greet them.

Ekman has been a prominent expert in emotion and facial expressions. The characters in Pixar's animated movie *Inside Out* were largely based on his breakdown of basic emotions. The fictional Dr. Lightman in the TV series *Lie to Me* is based on Ekman himself.[9]

How Does It Work?

There are two main ways to analyze facial expressions. One uses facial EMG (electromyography), placing small sensors directly on face muscles to measure even tiny contractions (like the subtle muscle movement for a frown).

The more common approach uses cameras. In contrast to the original method of human expert analysis, today it's more common to use a camera (sometimes just a webcam) and software algorithms to analyze changes in facial landmarks (like eyebrow position or lip curvature). The software can classify expressions into basic emotions like happiness, surprise, anger, etc., or provide continuous measures of positive/negative feeling (valence) and intensity (arousal).

Facial expression analysis can even be performed on multiple individuals at once, e.g., a group of people viewing a movie trailer.

What Can You Learn?

Facial expression analysis is widely used to evaluate emotional responses to advertising, video content, or product experiences. Did that funny commercial actually make people smile? Facial coding can tell you by tracking smiles moment-by-moment. Did a suspenseful scene in a trailer trigger surprise (raised eyebrows, widened eyes)? Yes, it can measure that.

This technique is particularly useful for getting unfiltered emotional reactions that consumers might not verbalize. It provides a readout of emotional valence and its timing during the stimulus.

Advantages

Expression analysis directly assesses emotional valence. A smile means positive, a frown means negative. That's intuitive information you don't get from GSR or heart rate alone. Using a camera can be non-intrusive and highly scalable. Hundreds of people can participate remotely just using their webcams. Facial coding gives real-time, second-by-second feedback on emotions.

Disadvantages

Automated facial coding via camera isn't as precise as sensor-based or human expert methods and might miss subtle expressions or misclassify them, especially with poor lighting. People can sometimes consciously fake or suppress expressions, although involuntary microexpressions are harder to disguise. The technology is best at detecting basic emotions; more complex states like pride or nostalgia are harder to spot. Cultural differences can also influence how much emotion people display on their face. Some individuals may show little change in expression while consuming content, even if they find it funny or disturbing.

Facial Expression Analysis: The Bottom Line

Facial EMG tends to be used mainly in academic labs. Commercial neuromarketing overwhelmingly uses automated facial coding via video or webcams. Both can offer useful information about emotional responses.

fNIRS: fMRI Light

Functional Near-Infrared Spectroscopy, or fNIRS, is a more recent addition to the neuromarketing toolkit. Think of it as a portable, light-based cousin to fMRI.

How Does fNIRS Work?

fNIRS shines near-infrared light into the head. The light is absorbed differently depending on the oxygenation level of the blood in the brain. Since active brain areas use more oxygen and get more blood flow, fNIRS can detect these changes to infer neural activity. Sensors are placed on the scalp, often in a headband or cap. fNIRS tracks blood flow changes like fMRI but only for areas near the brain's surface, up to about an inch deep.

What Can You Learn?

fNIRS is useful for monitoring activity in the prefrontal cortex, the part of the brain linked to attention, decision-making, and valuation.

It's particularly suited for studies in more natural settings where participants can move around a bit, like walking through a mock store or sitting upright using a computer. For example, researchers could use an fNIRS headband to see how activity in the prefrontal cortex changes as shoppers view different product displays.

Advantages

fNIRS is portable brain imaging. It's much smaller and more accessible than fMRI, allowing researchers to get neural data outside a traditional lab and in more realistic environments. It offers decent spatial resolution for cortical areas and is better than standard EEG for "where" on the brain's surface. Its temporal resolution is also faster than fMRI (hundreds of milliseconds vs. seconds). It's far more comfortable (and quiet!) for participants compared to fMRI.

Disadvantages

fNIRS only measures activity near the brain's surface. It cannot detect signals from deeper brain regions linked to raw emotion or memory, areas which fMRI can access. The spatial detail is also lower than fMRI. Signals can be affected by outside light, changes in skin blood flow, or even hair blocking the sensors. Since its use in neuromarketing is newer, the analysis standards and interpretation for marketing are less established than for EEG or fMRI.

fNIRS: The Bottom Line

fNIRS is still emerging in consumer research, having been used more in academia and fields like human factors research. Commercial use by marketers is limited but growing, often for specialized projects requiring portability.

MEG and PET: Powerful but Uncommon

There are a couple of other neuroimaging techniques you might hear about, but they are either rarely used or largely impractical for neuromarketing research: Magnetoencephalography (MEG) and Positron Emission Tomography (PET).

Magnetoencephalography

MEG detects the magnetic fields produced by brain activity. It has excellent temporal resolution like EEG and better spatial localization than EEG because magnetic fields aren't distorted by the skull. Unfortunately, MEG machines are incredibly expensive and require special shielded rooms. This makes MEG usage almost exclusively academic.

Positron Emission Tomography

PET scans involve injecting a radioactive tracer to measure metabolic activity in the brain. It can map activity in deep brain structures. However, PET is invasive, very expensive, and has poor temporal resolution. For ethical and practical reasons, PET is not used in neuromarketing studies on healthy subjects.

The Big Picture: Integrated Platforms

Neuromarketing studies are increasingly moving away from using just one tool for a project. The trend is toward integrated platforms that combine multiple technologies simultaneously.

How Does It Work?

Software platforms (like iMotions or GRAIL) allow researchers to synchronize and analyze data streams from different devices—perhaps eye tracking, EEG, GSR, and facial coding—all at the same time during the same study. Surveys and questionnaires can add information about the subjects' conscious beliefs and intentions.

What Can You Learn?

Combining tools provides a multi-dimensional view. Eye tracking shows *what* they looked at, EEG shows *when* their brain was engaged or paying attention, GSR shows *how intensely* they reacted, and facial coding shows if that reaction was *positive or negative*. By lining up all this data, you can get a much richer, more reliable picture of the consumer experience than any single tool could provide.

Advantages

With multiple tools, you get a holistic understanding and can triangulate findings. This overcomes the limitations of individual tools (e.g., combining GSR/HR with facial coding clarifies valence). It streamlines experiments and analysis compared to running separate studies. Eye tracking is often a particularly valuable enhancement for other methods since it reveals what subjects were looking at when there was some sort of emotional spike or decline in interest.

In general, more data streams are better. At one point, Nielsen Neuroscience said in their presentations that each method added to a study increased the predictive power. Even old-fashioned surveys boosted accuracy by a few percent.

Disadvantages

Using multiple tools increases complexity in data analysis and requires expertise across multiple methods. There's also a higher initial investment for the platform and multiple pieces of hardware. Ultimately, the cost for a study is higher. Generally, these are done in a lab setting.

Integrated Platforms: The Bottom Line

The use of integrated platforms is increasing because marketers want more comprehensive insights and budgets allow. It represents an evolution toward more holistic assessments of consumer responses.

Classic Neuromarketing

So there you have it—a look inside the classic neuromarketing insights toolkit. These technologies offer unique ways to understand the subconscious drivers of consumer behavior and to better predict their future actions.

Until the last few years, these tools were used mainly by big brands studying big projects—major ad campaigns, package redesign, rebranding, etc. As we learned in Part 2, variations on these methods have become far more widely available and economical.

Even these traditional methods have become somewhat more accessible from agencies and hardware/software vendors. If you aren't getting the insights you need from remote tools and wearables, see if one or more of these fit in your budget.

Notes

Chapter 1

1. https://www.goodreads.com/quotes/878561-the-mind-is-divided-like-a-rider-on-an-elephant
2. Aron, A., Badre, D., Brett, M., et al. (2007, November 14). *Politics and the brain* [Letter to the editor]. *The New York Times*.
3. Straits Research. (n.d.). *Neuromarketing market size, share & trends analysis report by technology, end-use industry, region and forecast, 2025–2033* (Report Code SRTE1726DR). Retrieved July 31, 2025, from https://straitsresearch.com/report/neuromarketing-market
4. Dooley, R. (2020, September 7). *Nielsen Makes Major Neuromarketing Cuts Due To Pandemic*. Forbes. https://www.forbes.com/sites/rogerdooley/2020/09/07/nielsen-neuromarketing-cuts/

Chapter 2

1. Gervais, S., Holland, A., and Dodd, M. (2013). My eyes are up here: the nature of the objectifying gaze toward women. *Sex Roles*. 69: 557–570. https://doi.org/10.1007/s11199-013-0316-x.
2. Business Insider. (2011, July). *Eye-tracking study reveals interesting differences in how men and women look at websites. Business Insider*. Retrieved from https://www.businessinsider.com/eye-tracking-study-2011-7

Chapter 4

1. Rancati, G., Ghosh, K., and Barraza, J. (2025). The contagion of neurologic immersion predicts retail purchases. *Frontiers in Neuroscience* 19: 1533784. https://doi.org/10.3389/fnins.2025.1533784
2. Dooley, R. (n.d.). *Passionistas* [Blog post]. Neuromarketing. Retrieved August 3, 2025, from *https://www.neurosciencemarketing.com/blog/articles/passionistas.htm*
3. Zak, P. J. (2020, October 1). Neurological correlates allow us to predict human behavior. *The Scientist*. Retrieved August 3, 2025, from https://www.the-scientist.com/neurological-correlates-allow-us-to-predict-human-behavior-67948/
4. Ibid.

Chapter 5

1. Blanton, H., Jaccard, J., Klick, J. et al. (2009). Strong claims and weak evidence: reassessing the predictive validity of the iat. *Journal of Applied Psychology* 94 (3): 567–582. https://doi.org/10.1037/a0014665.
2. Tierney, J. (2008, November 18). *A shocking test of bias* [Blog post]. TierneyLab. *The New York Times*. Retrieved August 3, 2025, from *https://archive.nytimes.com/tierneylab.blogs.nytimes.com/2008/11/18/a-shocking-test-of-bias/*
3. Project Implicit. (n.d.). *Take a test* [Web page]. Project Implicit. Retrieved August 3, 2025, from *https://implicit.harvard.edu/implicit/takeatest.html*
4. *Implicit Association Test* [Experiment guide]. Testable. Retrieved August 3, 2025, from https://www.testable.org/experiment-guides/attitudes/implicit-association-test/
5. Millisecond Software, LLC. (n.d.). *Implicit Association Test* [Test library page]. Millisecond. Retrieved August 3, 2025, from *https://www.millisecond.com/download/library/iat/*
6. GitHub. (n.d.). *Search results: "implicit association test"* [Web page]. GitHub. Retrieved August 3, 2025, from *https://github.com/search?q=implicit%20association%20test&type=repositories*

Chapter 6

1. VR-EEG: iMotions Next-Level Neuromarketing Research. (2021, April 29). Retrieved from https://www.researchgate.net/institution/iMotions/post/VR-EEG-iMotions-Next-Level-Neuromarketing-Research-6087f91cafd6e63fd0222963
2. Neurons Inc. (n.d.). Neuromarketing examples. Retrieved August 5, 2025, from https://www.neuronsinc.com/neuromarketing/examples

Chapter 7

1. Shu, L.L., Mazar, N., Gino, F. et al. (2012). RETRACTED: Signing at the beginning makes ethics salient and decreases dishonest self-reports in comparison to signing at the end. *Proceedings of the National Academy of Sciences USA* 109 (38): 15197–15200, https://doi.org/10.1073/pnas.1209746109.
2. Kuka, V. (2024, September 27). Role prompting: guide LLMs with persona-based tasks. Learn Prompting. https://learnprompting.org/docs/advanced/zero_shot/role_prompting
3. Ferrara, E. (2023). Bias in AI models: origins, impact, and mitigation strategies. ResearchGate. Retrieved from https://www.researchgate.net/publication/390115138_Bias_in_AI_Models_Origins_Impact_and_Mitigation_Strategies

Chapter 8

1. Penn, C. (2025, June 26). A first look at my new book, Almost Timeless: A free chapter. Christopher S. Penn. https://www.christopherspenn.com/2025/06/a-first-look-at-my-new-book-almost-timeless-a-free-chapter/
2. Sewell, C., & Brown, P. B. (2002). Customers for life: How to turn that one-time buyer into a lifetime customer. Crown Currency.
3. Clark, B., & Rieck, D. (2016). How to write magnetic headlines. Copyblogger. Retrieved August 5, 2025, from https://copyblogger.com/wp-content/uploads/2018/10/Copyblogger-How-to-Write-Magnetic-Headlines-2.pdf

Chapter 10

1. Iyer, J. (2023, December 4). Color psychology in visual design: A practical guide to impacting user behavior. UXmatters. Retrieved from https://www.uxmatters.com/mt/archives/2023/12/color-psychology-in-visual-design-a-practical-guide-to-impacting-user-behavior.php; Lischer, B. (n.d.). *Color psychology in branding: The persuasive power of color*. Ignyte. Retrieved from https://www.ignytebrands.com/the-psychology-of-color-in-branding/

Chapter 11

1. Lin, P.-Y., Grewal, N.S., Morin, C. et al. (2013). Oxytocin increases the influence of public service advertisements. *PLoS One 8* (2): e56934. https://doi.org/10.1371/journal.pone.0056934.
2. Fogg, B. J. (2009). *A behavior model for persuasive design*. Persuasive '09, Claremont, California, USA.
3. Fogg, B.J. (May 2002). "Stanford Guidelines for Web Credibility." A Research Summary from the Stanford Persuasive Technology Lab. Stanford University. www.webcredibility.org/guidelines

Chapter 12

1. Ariely, D., Loewenstein, G., and Prelec, D. (2006). "Coherent Arbitrariness": stable demand curves without stable preferences. In: *The Construction of Preference* (ed. S. Lichtenstein and P. Slovic), 246–270. Cambridge: Cambridge University Press.

Chapter 15

1. Montemayor, C., Halpern, J., and Fairweather, A. (2022). *In principle obstacles for empathic AI: why we can't replace human empathy in healthcare. AI & Society* 37 (4): 1353–1359. https://doi.org/10.1007/s00146-021-01230-z.

2. Knutsen, T. (2023, March 22). *AI lacks empathy: Artificial intelligence's emotional blindspot and the risk that it poses*. AI Consequences. Retrieved July 31, 2025, from https://aiconsequences.com/ai-lacks-empathy/
3. Heritage, S. (2025, July 12). "I felt pure, unconditional love": The people who marry their AI chatbots. *The Guardian*. Retrieved July 31, 2025, from https://www.theguardian.com/tv-and-radio/2025/jul/12/i-felt-pure-unconditional-love-the-people-who-marry-their-ai-chatbots/
4. Heinz, M. .V., Mackin, D. .M., Trudeau, B. .M. et al. (2025, March 27). Randomized trial of a generative AI chatbot for mental health treatment. *NEJM AI 2* (4): https://doi.org/10.1056/AIoa2400802.
5. Eaton, K. (2025, June 9). Why Duolingo's founder is doing damage control after AI announcement. Inc. Retrieved July 31, 2025, from https://www.inc.com/kit-eaton/why-duolingos-founder-is-doing-damage-control-after-ai-announcement/91199921
6. *Empathy Could Save U.S. Companies $180 Billion in Employee Retention Costs*. (2025, June 18). Businessolver. https://businessolver.com/news/empathy-could-save-u-s-companies-180-billion-in-employee-retention-costs/
7. Van Bommel, T. (2021, September 14). *Empathic leaders drive employee engagement and innovation*. Catalyst. https://www.catalyst.org/about/newsroom/2021/empathic-leaders-drive-employee-engagement
8. Dooley, R. (2024, June 23). *Carnival Cruise Line's loyalty program changes may be a costly mistake*. Forbes. https://www.forbes.com/sites/rogerdooley/2024/06/23/carnival-cruise-lines-loyalty-program-changes-may-be-a-costly-mistake/
9. Dooley, R. (2025, May 29). *Southwest Airlines just made a costly mistake in consumer psychology*. Forbes. https://www.forbes.com/sites/rogerdooley/2025/05/29/southwest-airlines-just-made-a-costly-mistake-in-consumer-psychology/
10. Goleman, D. (2006). *Social Intelligence: The New Science of Human Relationships*. New York: Bantam Books.
11. Schlegel, K., Sommer, N.R., and Mortillaro, M. (2025). Large language models are proficient in solving and creating emotional intelligence tests. *Communications Psychology 3* (1): Article 80. https://doi.org/10.1038/s44271-025-00258-x.

12. Rubin, M., Li, J.Z., Zimmerman, F. et al. (2025). Comparing the value of perceived human versus AI-generated empathy. *Nature Human Behaviour* https://doi.org/10.1038/s41562-025-02247-w.

Chapter 16

1. Carnival Cruise Line. (2025, September 15). *Carnival announces enhancements to new Carnival Rewards™ loyalty program for Diamond and Platinum guests.* Carnival News. https://www.carnival-news.com/2025/09/15/carnival-announces-enhancements-to-new-carnival-rewardsTM-loyalty-program-for-diamond-and-platinum-guests

Appendix

1. McClure, S.M., Li, J., Tomlin, D. et al. (2004). Neural correlates of behavioral preference for culturally familiar drinks. *Neuron* 44 (2): 379–387. https://doi.org/10.1016/j.neuron.2004.09.019.
2. Knutson, B., Rick, S., Wimmer, G.E. et al. (2007). Neural predictors of purchases. *Neuron* 53 (1): 147–156. https://doi.org/10.1016/j.neuron.2006.11.010.
3. Venkatraman, V., Dimoka, A., Pavlou, P.A. et al. (2015). Predicting advertising success beyond traditional measures: new insights from neurophysiological methods and market response modeling. *Journal of Marketing Research* 52 (4): 436–452. https://doi.org/10.1509/jmr.13.0593 (Original work published 2015).
4. Bennett, C.M., Baird, A.A., Miller, M.B., and Wolford, G.L. (2010). Neural correlates of interspecies perspective taking in the post-mortem Atlantic Salmon: An argument for proper multiple comparisons correction. *Journal of Serendipitous and Unexpected Results 1* (1): 1–5.
5. Oullier, O. (2012). Clear up this fuzzy thinking on brain scans. *Nature* 483: 7. https://doi.org/10.1038/483007a.
6. https://imotions.com/blog/learning/product-guides/eeg-cap/
7. https://stanford.edu/group/spanlab/Press/bk091007press.html
8. https://www.eyelogicsolutions.com/history-behind-eye-tracking/
9. Ekman, P. (n.d.). *Paul Ekman.* Paul Ekman Group Retrieved June 13, 2025, from https://www.paulekman.com/about/paul-ekman/.

Acknowledgments

Writing a book about the intersection of behavioral science, neuroscience, and AI feels a bit like assembling a puzzle while blindfolded—you need a lot of help to see the full picture. I've been fortunate to have extraordinary guides along the way.

First and foremost, my deepest gratitude goes to Robert Cialdini, who appears in these pages more than any other expert. Bob has been unfailingly helpful over the years, and his groundbreaking work on the principles of influence forms the bedrock of so much of what we know about persuasion.

Special thanks to Chris Penn, my go-to resource for deep AI thinking, whose insights pepper this book. Ideas like his "add a banana" concept and his exploring the unexpected corners of AI capability have added great value.

I'm deeply grateful to Paul Zak, whose research, particularly on oxytocin and trust, has illuminated so much about how we connect, trust, and buy.

This book stands on the shoulders of giants in behavioral science. My appreciation to the late Daniel Kahneman for showing us how we really think, BJ Fogg for the elegant power of the Behavior Model, Dan Ariely for surprising us with powerful insights from simple experiments, Richard Thaler for the nudge that changed everything.

Add to those luminaries the dozens of scientists, marketers, sales gurus, and others I've mentioned as resources with valuable insights.

I hope the mentions help spread their ideas far and wide. I know my readers will find those ideas as valuable as I have.

My LinkedIn community deserves recognition for providing an endless stream of insights. Your engagement, comments, and shares taught me more about what resonates than any textbook could.

To my publisher, editors, and production team—thank you for helping transform a manuscript into something people might actually want to read.

To the AI pioneers who have built and evolved models like ChatGPT, Claude, Gemini, and so many other general and specialized tools. Most of the ideas, tactics, and strategies I describe in Parts 3 and 4 of this book could not have existed two years ago.

Finally, the home team who makes everything possible.

To my wife Carol, who has graciously tolerated the closed office door and the glow of monitors at all times of the day and night. Thank you for your patience, your support, and for occasionally reminding me that not everyone finds obscure cognitive biases as fascinating as I do.

To our children, Alicia and Brian, both accomplished marketers in their own right, always ready to share interesting ideas and let me know when I'm wrong. And to my grandson Andrew, who served as my digital marketing intern during the writing of this book and shows great promise as an AI-native marketer.

To everyone mentioned here and the many others who contributed ideas, feedback, and encouragement along the way—this book is as much yours as it is mine. Any insights are shared; any errors are totally my own.

About the Author

Roger Dooley is a globally recognized expert in applying neuroscience and behavioral science to marketing, persuasion, and customer experience. His best-selling book *Brainfluence* has been translated into 11 languages, and *Friction* was named a Top 3 Management book by *strategy+business*. He writes at Forbes.com and hosts the *Brainfluence* podcast with more than 400 episodes. Roger created The Persuasion Slide™ framework for understanding customer behavior. He co-founded and sold College Confidential, the leading college-bound website. Roger is based in Austin, where he conducts important field research on breakfast tacos and BBQ brisket. Learn more at www.rogerdooley.com.

Index

Numerics
The 10X Rule (Cardone), 57
1988 *SPIN Selling* (Rackham), 57

access scarcity, 158
action, purpose, expectation (APE), 66
advanced AI behavioral techniques
   B2B behavioral differences, 166–167
   Behavioral Prompt Library, 171–172
   competitive behavioral analysis, 168–171
   food fight, 164–165
   mobile-specific behavioral psychology, 165–166
   multi-expert panels, 161–164
AI behavioral science dream team. 47–62
   errors, 51–52
   generic prompting, 49, 50
   headline suggestions, 49
   pattern matching, 49, 50
   role prompting, 59–62
   team prompting, 57–58
   testing your team, 58–59
AI-driven chatbots, 177, 186, 187
AI eye tracking simulators, 21–24
AI misuse, 51–52, 92, 208–209
   overconfidence in outputs, 51–52
   hallucinations, 51–52
   ethical risks, 92, 208–209
AI-powered emotional personalization, 202
AI-powered empathy check, 193–194

AI prompts
   action, purpose, expectation (APE), 66
   advantages, 89–90
   attention, interest, desire, action (AIDA), 66
   customer profile framework, 72–76
   dark patterns, 92
   "deep research" tools, 77–79
   feedback loop, 87–88
   gap-filling framework, 76–77
   industry analyst, 80–83
   interview approach, 74–76
   iteration approach, 77
   meta-prompting, 69–71
   multiplier effect, 90
   persistent knowledge, 84
   persuasion control center, 92–94
   projects and custom GPTs, 84–86
   reusing and updating information, 84–87
   role, action, context, execute/expectation (RACE), 66
   rules of thumb
      be ridiculously specific, 67
      give AI everything at the start, 68
      introduce the unexpected, 69
      Kaizen Your AI, 69
      save your best prompts, 68–69
      trust but verify, 68
   share your knowledge, 71–72
   strategic prompting, 76–77
   task, action, goal (TAG), 67
   understanding business and brand, 73

AI prompts (*continued*)
   understanding industry ecosystem, 73–74
   updating marketing successes and failures, 83–84
AIDA framework. *See* attention, interest, desire, action (AIDA)
Amazon, 12, 127, 141, 151
analysis paralysis. *See* choice paradox; cognitive overload
anchoring effect
   anchoring mistakes, 145
   overview, 145
   pricing page with five choices, 146
anti-trust signals, 136–137
Apple Vision Pro, 43
Ariely, Dan, 53, 56, 103, 132, 145
artificial scarcity, 155–156
attention, interest, desire, action (AIDA), 66
attention and emotional response
   cognitive load check, 112
   cognitive momentum, 123
   color science, 115–116
   creating information gap, 116–117
   curiosity gap prompt, 124
   emotional triggers, 118–122
   feedback loop, 124
   F-pattern, 114
   pattern interruption, 117–118
   scroll-tracking tools, 123
   visual complexity, 114–115
   zero mental translation, 113
   Z-pattern, 114
"audit" prompt, 97
authentic scarcity, 155–156
authority, 102, 105, 106, 133–134, 137, 158, 162

B2B behavioral differences, 166–167
Baer, Jay, 54
Barrett, Lisa Feldman, 122
behavioral economics/behavioral science experts
   Ariely, Dan, 53, 56, 103, 132, 145
   Berger, Jonah, 53
   Cialdini, Robert, 7, 48, 51–53, 58, 60, 68, 70, 92, 95, 104, 105, 132, 162
   Eyal, Nir, 53–54
   Fogg, B.J, 48, 53, 58, 70, 95, 103, 128–130, 162
   Harhut, Nancy, 54
   Kahneman, Daniel, 7, 48, 50, 51, 53, 58, 61, 70, 95, 101, 103, 117, 162
   Shotton, Richard, 54
   Sunstein, Cass, 54
   Thaler, Richard, 53
Behavioral Prompt Library, 171–172
   categories, 171
   editing, 172
   improvement tracking, 171
   prompt templates, 171
   usage tips, 172
behavioral science for all, 5–6. *See also* behavioral economist
   AI dream team, 47–62
   principles, 52–54
Berger, Jonah, 53
Bezos, Jeff, 162, 163
biometric measurements
   common biometric measurements, 29
   Immersion Neuroscience (*see* Immersion Neuroscience)
   overview, 29
   wearables, 29–31
Bliss, Jeanne, 54
blood oxygen measurement, 30
bonus scarcity, 158
brain wave measurement. *See* electroencephalography (EEG)
Brainfluence (Dooley), 241
breathing rate measurement, 29–30
Brown, Brené, 189

Caldwell, Leigh, 56
call to action (CTA), 102–105, 108, 114, 134, 142, 162, 163

Canva, 22
Cardone, Grant, 57
Carnegie, Dale, 56
Carnival loyalty program, 197
caution on all-knowing AI, 51–52
Celebrity Cruises, 180
The Challenger Sale (Dixon), 57
ChatGPT, 7, 15, 50, 52, 57, 68, 71, 82, 85–86, 104, 107, 112–115, 117–119, 122, 131, 146–148, 154, 164, 165, 172, 203
   custom GPTs, 84–85
   generic call-to-action, 98
   under-leveraged social proof, 98
   vague value proposition, 98
choice architecture, 149–150
choice paradox, 141–143
Cialdini, Robert, 7, 48, 51–53, 58, 60, 68, 70, 92, 95, 104, 105, 132, 162
Cialdini's seven principles of influence, 48, 50, 51, 104, 105, 124
   authority, 133–134
   commitment and consistency, 134–136
   reciprocity, 98, 134–135, 170
   scarcity, 151–160
   social proof, 105–108, 132
   unity, 51, 68
Claude, 7, 15, 52, 59, 85–88, 96–99, 103, 153–156, 167, 168, 170, 172, 183, 185, 186, 190, 195, 203
   emotional and empathy analysis, 186–187, 190, 195
   hitting "Retry," 99
   iterative refinement, 97–99
cognitive empathy, 185
cognitive overload, 111–112, 141–143
color associations, 115
color science, 115–116
communication with customers
   emotional intelligence, 4, 28, 186–187, 201–202, 207–210
   empathy (*see* empathy)
competitive behavioral analysis, 168–171
competitive intelligence urgency, 167

Confessions of the Pricing Man: How Price Affects Everything (Simon), 56
Contagious, Invisible Influence (Berger), 53
The Convenience Revolution (Hyken), 54
conversion friction, 111–115, 141–145
   cognitive overload, 111–112
   choice overload, 141–143
   visual complexity, 114–115
   zero mental translation, 113
conversion optimization, 59–61, 70, 103–104
copywriting & communication experts
   Handley, Ann, 55
   Heath, Chip, 55
   Heath, Dan, 55
   Luntz, Frank, 55
   Ogilvy, David, 55
   Schwartz, Eugene, 55
   Sugarman, Joseph, 55
   Wiebe, Joanna, 55
Covey, Stephen M., 129, 130
COVID-19 pandemic, 6–7
crisis communication, 199–201
   empathy failures, 178–183
   emotionally intelligent messaging, 199–201
   stakeholder communication, 205
cross-cultural emotional AI, 208
Cruising, 179
The Cult of the Customer (Hyken), 54
cultural sensitivity check, 204
curiosity gap prompt, 124
customer anger, 178–183, 199–201
   empathy failures, 178–183
   crisis communication, 199–201
customer experience (CX) experts
   Baer, Jay, 54
   Bliss, Jeanne, 54
   Dixon, Matthew, 54
   Hyken, Shep, 54
   Reichheld, Fred, 54

customer-facing communications
   crisis communications, 201
   internal communications, 200–201
   policy changes, 199–200
   recovery messages, 200
   service disruptions, 199
customer insights, 3, 30, 75, 118
customer profile framework
   customer goals, 72, 75
   decision journey, 72, 76
   demographics & psychographics, 72, 75
   emotional drivers, 72–73, 76
customer reaction predictor, 204

Damasio, Antonio, 119
decision architecture
   anchoring effect, 145–147
   choice paradox, 141–143
   decoy effect, 143–144
   defaults, 144–145
   loss framing vs. gain framing, 147–148
   prevention-oriented products, 147, 148
   promotion-oriented products, 147, 148
   temporal framing, 148–149
decoy effect, 143–144, 150
"deep research" tools, 77–79
   customer profiles creation, 78–79
democratized neuromarketing, 7–8, 21–24, 47–49
   AI as enabler, 7, 47–49
   low-cost tools, 21–24
device camera eye tracking, 14–15
digital course, 155–156
digital trust, 128–129
Dixon, Matthew, 54, 57, 112, 167
Duolingo, 178

"The Early Bird Design Plan," 157
ECG. *See* electrocardiogram (ECG)
EEG. *See* electroencephalography (EEG)
The Effortless Experience (Dixon), 54, 112
Ekman, Paul, 226

electrocardiogram (ECG), 29
   advantages, 223
   description, 222
   disadvantages, 223
   findings, 223
electrodermal activity (EDA). *See* galvanic skin response (GSR)
electroencephalography (EEG)
   advantages, 217
   description, 41, 216
   disadvantages, 217–218
   findings, 217
   hardware progress, 42
elephant and rider metaphor, 3
emotional blindspot, 177, 183
emotional drivers, 76, 119, 121
emotional empathy, 185
emotional intelligence, 4, 28, 186–187, 208, 209. *See also* empathy
   personalized emotional intelligence, 201–202
   predictive emotional intelligence, 207–208
emotionally intelligent business
   cross-cultural emotional AI, 208
   multimodal empathy, 208
   predictive emotional intelligence, 207–208
emotional multiplier effect, 184–185
emotional triggers, 122
   build on what you've learned, 120
   customer's emotional drivers analysis, 119
   get more powerful insights with deep research, 120–121
Emotiv, 42
empathy, 4
   AI-powered emotional personalization, 202
   AI-powered empathy check, 193–194
   audit, 191–192, 196, 197
   cognitive empathy, 185
   cultural sensitivity check, 204
   customer-facing communications, 199–201
   deep emotional betrayal, 182

emotional blindspot, 177, 183
emotional connection with brand, 179
emotional empathy, 185
and emotional intelligence, 4, 186–187, 201–202, 207–210
emotionally intelligent business, 207–208
emotional multiplier effect, 184–185
empathy gap, 184
ethical implications, 208–210
failures, 178, 181, 183, 185
feedback to AI, 205
in humans, 178, 186–187
motivational empathy, 185
permanent debarkation, 182
rewriter, 204
segment-specific empathy, 201–202
60-second emotion check, 189–191
spotting emotional pitfalls, 205–206
stakeholder-specific communication, 205
starter prompts, 203–205
transactional loyalty, 181–182
empathy gap, 184
endowment effect, 103, 104
Everybody Writes (Handley), 55
expertise scarcity, 158
"expert systems," 15
Eyal, Nir, 53–54
eye tracking, 34, 231
AI eye tracking simulators, 19–24
book cover thumbnail experiment, 12–14, 16–17
device camera eye tracking, 14–15
eye-trackers
advantages, 220
description, 218–219
disadvantages, 220
findings, 219
gaze paths, 11
heat maps, 11, 15, 16
intense color, 11
opacity maps, 11
overview, 11
remote eye tracking, 17–19
webcam-based eye tracking, 27

facial action coding system (FACS), 25
advantages, 227
description, 226–227
disadvantages, 227–228
findings, 227
overview, 226
facial coding, 34
facial action coding system (FACS) (*see* facial action coding system (FACS))
implementation, 27–28
limitations, 26–27
microexpressions, 25, 226
remote, real time facial coding, 25–26
facial EMG (electromyography), 226
facial expression analysis. *See* facial action coding system (FACS)
FACS. *See* facial action coding system (FACS)
false precision, 22–23, 34
limits of eye-tracking simulators, 22–23
biometric over-interpretation, 34
"Father of Modern Advertising." *See* Ogilvy, David
fear of missing out (FOMO), 160, 167
Feng-GUI, 23
fitness trackers, 29, 211
five-minute behavioral audit, 95–97
high-impact behavioral hurdles diagnosis, 96
prioritizing the issues, 96
recommending concrete revision per issue, 96
fMRI. *See* functional magnetic resonance imaging (fMRI)
fNIRS. *See* functional near-infrared spectroscopy (fNIRS)
Fogg, B.J, 48, 53, 58, 70, 95, 103, 128–130, 162
Fogg Behavior Model, 128

Forbes, 182
Foreman, George, 137
"F-pattern," 114
"fresh start effect," 98
Friction (Dooley), 53–54
functional magnetic resonance imaging (fMRI)
    advantages, 215
    controversies, 214
    description, 214
    disadvantages, 215
    findings, 215
functional near-infrared spectroscopy (fNIRS)
    advantages, 229
    description, 228
    disadvantages, 229
    findings, 228–229

galvanic skin response (GSR), 231
    advantages, 221
    description, 221
    disadvantages, 222
    findings, 221
gap-filling framework, 76–77
Gemini, 52, 71, 103, 121, 132, 135, 137, 138, 142–144, 146, 149, 157, 158, 162, 164, 165, 172, 195–197
    choice overload/analysis paralysis, 99
    cognitive overload, 99
    deep research applications, 138–139, 142–145
    loss aversion is missing, 99
    paradox of choice, 99
    social proof and specificity, 99
    vague value proposition, 99
Gemini Gems, 86
Github, 39
Gladwell, Malcolm, 38
Gobé, Mark, 119
Godin, Seth, 118, 162
Goleman, Daniel, 189
"good *vs.* good enough" tradeoff, 17
GPT-4 identical expert prompts, 59, 186

Grok, 52
GSR. *See* galvanic skin response (GSR)
gut reactions. *See* implicit tests

Haidt, Jonathan, 3
Handbook on Psychology of Pricing (Husemann-Kopetzky), 56
Handley, Ann, 55, 57
Harhut, Nancy, 54
Harvard Implicit Association Test, 38
Hatfield, Elaine, 122
Hayward, Tony, 201
heart rate variability (HRV). *See* electrocardiogram (ECG)
Heath, Chip, 55
Heath, Dan, 55
homepage optimization, 102–105, 111–118, 128–136
    attention sequencing, 111–118
    call-to-action visibility, 102–105
    visual complexity reduction, 114–115
    trust signals, 128–136
homo economicus, 179
Hooked: How to Build Habit-Forming Products (Eyal), 53
How to Win Friends and Influence People (Carnegie), 56
Huey, Edmund B., 218
Hug Your Haters (Baer), 54
Husemann-Kopetzky, Markus, 56
Hyken, Shep, 54

Ideogram, 68
"I Love You More Than My Dog" (Bliss), 54
Immersion Neuroscience
    applications, 32–33
    and eye tracking, 34
    and facial coding, 34
    "Immersion" metric, 32
    limitations of, 34
    setup, 33
    trust hormone measurement, 31

implicit tests
   advantages, 225
   applications, 39
   description, 224
   disadvantages, 225
   findings, 224–225
   implementation, 38–39
   limitations of, 38
industry context document creation
   competitive dynamics, 81
   customer psychology & behavior, 80–81
   industry language & culture, 81
   market landscape, 80
   reality check, 82–83
   sales & marketing dynamics, 81
   success factors & barriers, 81
   trends & disruptions, 81
industry ecosystem
   competitor positioning, 74
   emerging trends, 74
   industry language, 74
   market dynamics, 73
Influence: How and Why People Agree to Things (Cialdini), 51, 52
information gap, 116–117
integrated platforms, 230–232
interview approach, 74–76

James, Lebron, 133

Kahneman, Daniel, 7, 48, 50, 51, 53, 58, 61, 70, 95, 101, 103, 117, 162
Knutsen, Thomas, 177

Laja, Peep, 70
Luntz, Frank, 55, 57

machine learning, 7, 15, 20, 26, 42, 219
Made to Stick: Why Some Ideas Survive and Others Die (Heath and Heath), 55
magnetoencephalography (MEG), 230
Marci, Carl, 29
Massey, Brian, 70

Meta, 43
meta-prompting, 69–71
Meta Quest 3, 43
microcommitments, 134–136
microexpressions, 25, 226
Millisecond's Inquisit platform, 38
mobile-specific behavioral psychology, 165–166
motivational empathy, 185
multi-expert panels
   Bezos, Jeff (entrepreneurship, growth, leadership), 162
   Cialdini, Robert (influence principles), 162
   Fogg, B.J. (behavior design), 162
   Godin, Seth (modern marketing), 162
   Kahneman, Daniel (cognitive biases), 162
   novelty, 163
   recommendations, 163
   unified strategy, 162
multimodal empathy, 208
Muse, 42

Neuromarketing 2.0, 7–8, 41–43, 213–232
   accessibility for small businesses, 8, 21–24, 47–49
   contrast with classic neuromarketing, 6–7, 213–232
   definition, 7–8
Neurons Inc., 43
NeuroSky, 42
New England Journal of Medicine, 177
Nielsen Neuroscience, 7, 29, 231
non-conscious appeals, 4
NotebookLM, 86
Nova, 180
Nudge (Thaler), 53

Ogilvy, David, 55

Palmer, Melina, 56
panic/grief system, 119
Panksepp, Jaak, 119

pattern interruption, 117–118
Penn, Chris, 69
personalized emotional
    intelligence, 201–202
physical activity measurement, 30
positron emission tomography
    (PET), 230
Poundstone, William, 55–56
powerful brain mapping. *See* functional
    magnetic resonance
    imaging (fMRI)
Predictably Irrational (Ariely), 53
predictive emotional
    intelligence, 207–208
Pre-Suasion (Cialdini), 51
price anchoring, 145, 149
pricing page optimization, 141–150
    choice overload, 141–143
    anchoring strategies, 145–146
    decoy effect, 143–144
    loss vs. gain framing, 147–148
Priceless: The Myth of Fair Value
    (Poundstone), 55
pricing psychology audit, 149–150
pricing psychology & strategy experts
    Ariely, Dan, 56
    Caldwell, Leigh, 56
    Husemann-Kopetzky, Markus, 56
    Palmer, Melina, 56
    Poundstone, William, 55–56
    Simon, Hermann, 56
product launch messaging, 116–118,
    151–160
    curiosity gap, 116–117
    scarcity framing, 151–160
The Psychology of Price (Caldwell), 56
The Psychology of Selling (Tracy), 57

quantity scarcity, 157
quick win prompts
    "audit" prompt, 97
    call to action (CTA), 102–105, 108,
        114, 134, 142, 162, 163
    ChatGPT o4-mini, 98
    five-minute behavioral audit, 95–97
    "fresh start effect," 98
    gain frame, 101
    Gemini 2.5 Flash, 99
    Gemini 2.5 Pro, 99
    headline makeover, 101–102
    hitting "Retry" on AI model, 99
    loss frame, 101
    psychological failure points
        identification, 95–97
    social proof power-ups, 105–108
    stacking multiple triggers, 102

Rackham, Neil, 57
rational appeals, 4
real-time empathy coaching, 201
Reichheld, Fred, 54
remote, real time facial coding,
    25–26
remote eye tracking
    facial expression analysis, 19
    limitations of, 18
    for non-experts, 18–19
    phone-based eye tracking, 18
    technical setup, 19
    testing, 19
    webcam, 18
"Request More Information" call to
    action, 11–12
role, action, context, execute/
    expectation (RACE), 66
role prompting
    be specific about expertise, 59–60
    combine roles with clear tasks, 60
    don't lose your star players, 62
    multi-step refinement, 61–62
    prompt for questions, 60–61
    stay relevant, 61
    stereotypes and demographics
        avoidance, 61
    use "you are" instead of "act as," 60
    watch for hallucinations, 61
Royal Caribbean, 180–183
rules-based process, 15

sales experts
   Cardone, Grant, 57
   Carnegie, Dale, 56
   Dixon, Matt, 57
   Rackham, Neil, 57
   Tracy, Brian, 57
   Ziglar, Zig, 56
scarcity
   access scarcity, 158
   ad agencies using scarcity, 153–154
   authentic *vs.* artificial scarcity, 155–156
   bonus scarcity, 158
   ethical scarcity, 160
   expertise scarcity, 158
   fake scarcity, 152
   framing, 153–155
   heavy scarcity, 152
   in luggage brand, 154–155
   psychology of, 151–152
   quantity scarcity, 157
   with social proof, 159–160
   time scarcity, 152, 157
Schwartz, Eugene, 55
science-based triggers, 6
segment-specific empathy, 201–202
Sell or Be Sold (Cardone), 57
Shotton, Richard, 54
Silversea Cruises, 180–181, 190, 191, 195, 196
Simon, Hermann, 56
60-second emotion check, 189–191
skin conductance (SC). *See* galvanic skin response (GSR)
skin temperature measurement, 30
slow-motion video, 25
smartwatches, 29
social proof, 105–108, 132
   with scarcity, 159–160
specific experts, 58–59
stakeholder-specific messaging/ communication, 201, 205

strategic prompting, 76–77
Sugarman, Joseph, 55, 123
Sunstein, Cass, 54
Sutherland, Rory, 118

Talk Triggers (*Baer*), 54
task, action, goal (TAG), 67
team prompting, 57–58
Testable, 38
Thaler, Richard, 53
time scarcity, 152, 157
Tracy, Brian, 57
transactional loyalty, 181–182
trust
   anti-trust signals, 136–137
   audit, 129–131
   authority, 133
   digital trust, 128–129
   microcommitments, 134–136
   oxytocin levels, 128
   recommendations, 130
   repairing trust failures, 178–183
   social proof spectrum, 132–133
   transference strategies, 137–139
The Truth About Pricing (Palmer), 56

The Ultimate Question (Reichheld), 54
Unravel Research, 42
urgency, 156–157, 167

virtual and augmented reality, 42–43
visual complexity, 114–115
von Ahn, Luis, 178

wearables, biometric measurements
   advantages of, 30
   barriers, 30–31
   blood oxygen measurement, 30
   breathing rate measurement, 29–30
   electrocardiogram, 29
   fitness trackers, 29
   physical activity measurement, 30

wearables, biometric (*continued*)
    skin temperature measurement, 30
    smartwatches, 29
webcam-based eye tracking, 27
Whitman, Drew Eric, 118
Wiebe, Joanna, 55
Winning on Purpose (Reichheld), 54
Words That Work (Luntz), 55

Would You Do That to Your Mother? (Bliss), 54

Zak, Paul, 31, 128–130
zero mental translation, 113
Zero Price effect, 103
Ziglar, Zig, 56
Z-pattern, 114